GROUND
COVER
PLANTS

by the same author

GROUND COVER PLANTS

MARGERY FISH

B.T.BATSFORD · LONDON

First published in 1964 by
W. H. & L. Collingridge Limited, London
Reissued in 1970 by
David & Charles (Publishers) Limited
Published by Faber & Faber Limited in 1980
This edition published in 2002 by
B T Batsford
64 Brewery Road
London N7 9NT

A member of **Chrysalis** Books plc

ISBN 0 7134 8751 8

Printed and bound in Great Britain by Bell & Bain Ltd., Glasgow.

The publishers gratefully acknowledge the help of Marianne Williams,
Graham Rice and Sir Henry Boyd-Carpenter in preparing
this new edition of the book.

A CIP catalogue record for this book is available from the British Library.

Contents

Foreword

The use of ground cover plants has run through many phases. First it was developed as a response to the need to look after large borders and large gardens, both private and public: as labour became more scarce and more expensive, the plants took over the work.

This often led to the planting of uniform green swathes of foliage which, while certainly better than mulch, concrete or bare soil, could rarely be described as interesting or attractive.

Then came *Ground Cover Plants* in which Margery Fish moved on from this municipal approach and, recognising, as she put it, that 'a garden well clothed is more attractive than one in which there are vast expanses of bare soil', developed a ground covering approach in which the quality and interaction of the plants covering the ground is as important as their ability to restrict the growth of weeds and cover bare soil.

This book sparked a realisation amongst gardeners that successful ground cover did not depend on beds being planted with broad sweeps of a single variety, for while such an approach is valuable on roadside embankments in the garden we need plants which are far more than purely functional.

So Margery Fish made us aware that plants do not have to be dull, evergreen, spreading in habit or uncomfortably vigorous to perform the functional element of the ground covering task, that plants which are in themselves attractive and interesting can cover the ground effectively. So this book presents her choice of attractive ground covering plants suited to gardens rather than public parks.

Since the initial publication of this book in 1964, the increasingly widespread use of ground cover on roadsides and in the grounds of large country houses has rather tainted the ideal that Mrs Fish expounded so successfully. A hint of a sneer has grown up amongst gardeners as dissatisfaction with this intensely practical, 'plants as paving' approach to ground cover planting has tainted the more sophisticated vision discussed by Mrs Fish in this book.

Now, the reappearance of *Ground Cover Plants*, after a long absence from our bookshelves, will again rekindle the recognition that plants that naturally inhibit weed growth and cover the soil can also be beautiful. And, of course, we are again able to enjoy the amiable and accessible style with which Margery Fish lays out her case, recommending plants which experience in her garden at East Lambrook Manor proved to her really do combine elegance with effectiveness.

Graham Rice, 2002

Introduction

One of the innovations that is becoming almost universal in our changing ways of gardening is the use of ground cover.

Finding attractive plants to cover ground that would otherwise need endless work to keep it free of weeds originated, no doubt, from lack of labour. There is no question that in parts of the garden where there is a close-growing ground cover the plants take care of themselves. We know this in our own gardens. The flower beds furnished with large established clumps, which join up to make a solid bank of foliage and flower, give no trouble at all; it is the places where bare soil surrounds shrubs or newly planted seedlings that become weedy and need constant attention.

I am sure that ground cover helps the plants as well as the gardener. A thick cover of vegetation conserves moisture and most plants seem to do better when growing close to their neighbours than in isolation. After all this is nature's way. There is no bare soil in the wild; it is only man who keeps scratching away to keep clean the naked soil he has produced artificially.

From the aesthetic angle I think most gardeners agree that a garden well clothed is more attractive than one in which there are vast expanses of bare soil, and added beauty – by contrast or harmony – can be achieved by the use of plants of different colour, texture or form.

No one would suggest ground cover in a vegetable garden, which can be kept clean with hoe or cultivator, although even there I have seen a thick mulch of straw used with excellent results.

Visitors to my garden often ask how I manage to spread compost when there is no bare space to be seen. They probably see the garden in summer when everything is in full growth. In late autumn there are enough gaps between the plants for us to spread about 150 cubic feet of compost on about an acre of garden every year, working on the principle that soil growing so much must get back the equivalent of what it gives.

To enjoy ground cover without reservation it is important to find the right plants for every position (and start them in soil that is completely free of perennial weeds). Luckily, there are innumerable plants from which to choose.

~ 1 ~
Foliage Plants for Ground Cover

Some of the most spectacular ground cover is obtained by using plants with beautiful leaves, and if one can find plants that make good autumn colour some very rich effects can be obtained.

The most colourful of all the bergenias is undoubtedly Ballawley Hybrid*, and its leaves are bigger than any others. They are not, however, as tough as some of the others and if the plant is grown where it will catch the wind the great crimson leaves may be tumbled and bruised. But there are usually shady, sheltered places where it will be safe and it is worth taking trouble for such a wonderful plant. The leaves can be as wide as 10 inches across, they are very glossy and bright green for most of the year. But at the approach of winter they become rich dark crimson, liver coloured in fact. The stems that hold the large clusters of crimson flowers are red, and altogether the effect is most sumptuous just at the time when one needs colour most. After flowering the leaves become green again.

The next in size is *B. cordifolia*, especially the variety *B. c. purpurea**, which has very large leaves, rounded and crinkled at the edges. The ordinary form does not change colour so noticeably in winter although there is usually a tinge of red discernible round the edges. But in the purple form, which is the one the late Gertrude Jekyll used so extensively and is sometimes called Miss Jekyll's Form*, the leaves turn purple in winter with glints of crimson. The flowers of this bergenia are a deep magenta-pink, and are carried proudly on stems that can be 18 inches high.

The leaves of *B. crassifolia* are not as big or crinkled as those of *B. cordifolia*, but they are very bright and cheerful, spoon-shaped and glossy and most colourful in winter, turning wonderful shades of orange, crimson and mahogany. The colours are particularly telling on the rounded, shining leaves.

B.x schmidtii has rounded, fluttering leaves on longer stalks than in the other varieties, and I do not think it is such a good ground cover plant, but it is good for growing on banks, and with me it flowers earlier and more generously than the others. It colours occasionally but never as much or as regularly as the others.

There is more colour from the leaves of *B. delavayi** and *B. purpurascens* because the purple leaves are lined with crimson, but they grow in a different way, perking up so that the light can shine through the leaves and give them a ruby glow. They are not therefore such good ground cover plants, although the colour of the upright leaves is brilliant.

Bergenias are not the only members of the saxifrage family useful for ground cover. *Tellima grandiflora* is an American plant. Akin to heuchera, it grows from Alaska to California and has leaves which are among the most beautiful of any I know. They are round and hairy and are delightful shades of pink when they first unfurl in the spring. They become green by midsummer with dark etchings, and turn to crimson again in the autumn. This easy evergreen plant increases quite well, it is quite hardy and in early summer produces its 2-foot spikes of hanging green bells. After they have been out a week or so the bells develop a pink tinge and remain like that for several weeks. *T. g. purpurea* (*T. g. rubra*) is an even more colourful variation of this plant, with leaves that have a purplish tinge all through the year and become really brilliant in autumn and winter. The flowers of this tellima are more yellow than green. I have never found that the tellimas mind if they are planted in sun or shade. If asked for a decision I would say they are shade plants but will also grow in sun.

Almost richer in colour is *Heuchera rubescens*. The colour of the young leaves is old rose, and later they turn to coppery mahogany. As they age the colour is purplish with crimson tones. This plant grows close to the soil and makes flat rosettes from which arise short sprays of greenish-buff flowers.

I have been given other heucheras with bronzed leaves from time to time, but naming them is a different matter. One with brown-mahogany leaves has scented snuff-coloured flowers. *H. micrantha* is sometimes sold as *H. rubescens* but differs in the colour of its flowers, which are purple. The leaves of *H. richardsonii* are a rich red-brown and it has light brown flowers. Another with bronze leaves was sold to me as *H. hispida*.

Heucheras with dark green leaves are derived from *H. americana*, which has very dark green leaves, and *H. sanguinea*, with brilliant red flowers.

The foliage of *H. viridis* is very dark and hairy, it grows close to the soil and the leaves are more scalloped than some of the others. It is an excellent ground cover plant and has flowers the same pale green as tellima but without any trace of pink.

We used to call a cross between heuchera and tiarella *Heuchera tiarelloides* and that name describes the plant exactly. But now it must be known as *Heucherella tiarelloides*. Its leaves are among the most beautiful of any in the garden, having the delicate pointed shape of *Tiarella wherryi* and the pencillings of a heuchera. The leaves are pale green and the flowers pink in tufted sprays. *Heucherella* Bridget Bloom is a much more recent introduction, and is one of the best ground cover plants of recent years. It does best in shade and should flower from early May till late October. It has the fine upright growth of the tiarella, but with the vigour of the heuchera it is a much more reliable plant.

Tiarella wherryi is a most attractive plant for a moist situation, but it does not increase very fast and is therefore not so good for ground cover. But *T. cordifolia* has running roots and covers everything in sight in a short time. Though individually the plants have not the compact upright growth of *T. wherryi* the general effect is good. All the 'foam flowers' have fluffy heads of small cream flowers, and do best in shady soil that is not too dry.

Geranium atlanticum* is not evergreen but it makes its appearance at a time when good leaves are needed, and I would plant it in places that are normally bare in winter. For this bulbous geranium – from the Atlas Mountains and not the Atlantic seaboard as one might expect – has charming finely cut leaves in fresh green and they appear with the autumn rains. Nothing could be prettier than the carpet of ferny foliage instead of bare earth and the plant can be grown with other plants. Autumn crocuses are quite happy growing among the leaves, and when the leaves of the crocus are at their most luxuriant there is no competition from the geranium. *G. atlanticum* is quite dwarf, the carpet of leaves grows to about 6 inches and in the spring the bright blue flowers are carried on stalks about a foot high. These flowers are worthy of close scrutiny because they are veined with red, which gives the effect of shot silk.

Hostas that grow so well in the shade of a woodland garden are magnificent foliage plants, but they lose their leaves and have nothing to offer from autumn to late spring, although they make up for this lapse by the magnificence of their great leaves all through the summer.

Pulmonarias have something to offer all the time, in fact the only moment when the leaves are not quite so beautiful is when the plant is flowering, and this applies only to the more aristocratic varieties. The ordinary *P. officinalis* varies not at all, and its heart-shaped spotted leaves are big and luxuriant when the blue and pink flowers come out like hundreds and thousands. There is a form of this which has leaves that are practically silver, until the plant is in bloom when they are shrivelled and twisted. Directly the flowers are over this pulmonaria improves in plumage and for most of the year has narrow silver leaves which are lovely – in a quiet, refined way.

The best way to choose pulmonarias for ground cover is to pick them for their leaves. As a rule forms of *P. saccharata*, of which Mrs Moon is the best known, have very good leaves, long and very heavily spotted. Pulmonarias vary considerably and there are often interesting forms to be found in different gardens and nurseries, but it is not always easy to give them names. I have one given to me by a friend which has narrow leaves almost blue in colour, well spotted in the off season but usually rather plain when the plant is in flower. They are such a good colour that they would be welcome at any time with or without spots.

I would not recommend the deep blue pulmonarias for ground cover if they are to be planted by themselves, for they are deciduous and the leaves do not appear until flowering time, and then are rather small compared with the other varieties.

But *P. rubra* has luxuriant leaves and there will be no weeds where it grows. This plant has bright green foliage, rather on the pale side, but the leaves are large and hairy and make carpets of coarse rough green. It is well named the Christmas cowslip because the first bright flowers often open before Christmas, at a time when any colour is most welcome and the pure coral of this flower particularly so. For years I have grown *P. rubra* with all green leaves and recently I got hold of a red one, this time attributed to the late Mr Bowles, and with spotted instead of all-green leaves. The spots are not very distinct but the leaves are darker and more like the ordinary blue and pink pulmonarias.

Several members of the corydalis family are only too eager to cover all the ground in sight. On principle I have to discourage *C. lutea* because it becomes a nuisance if left to its own devices, but if there were spots in the garden that would otherwise be bare it would undoubtedly be delighted to cover them with delicate glaucous foliage and the effect would be very pretty. I have never managed to stop it filling cracks in walls and there I let it remain, but I encourage the pale flowered form in another part of the garden, but do not find it so eager to colonise. This one I have planted in good soil in my ditch garden, and though the parent plants stay with me so far there have been no children. Probably if I gave it poor soil and persecuted it as I do the common yellow form I should have all the seedlings I want.

Seeding seems to be a habit of the evergreen corydalis forms, although not so prolifically with the deciduous types. The ferny-leaved corydalis, well named *C. cheilanthifolia*, makes forests of little plants all round the parent plants, and they grow very quickly. The leaves are a warm brownish-green and a patch of the plant brings a welcome colour break into the garden. The flowers tone in well but are not very striking. All the same I have seen those delicate buff-green sprays used quite effectively in miniature floral arrangements. The purplish form of *C. cheilanthifolia* is a very pretty colour, soft pale pinkish tones of purple and lavender with flowers that tone. A friend of mine has a large paved rock garden and here this little corydalis seeds about and makes pretty carpets of palest pastel shades. For all their air of delicacy the corydalis family are not so fragile as they look. The stems may be slender and transparent and the finely cut leaves seem to have little substance, but they are tough little plants, not at all discouraged by neglect, brutality or cold weather.

Sweet Cicely, which is the country name for *Myrrhis odorata*, has very fern-like leaves too, they are fairly deep green and absolutely flat so that they cover the ground with delicate tracery in their early stages. Later on, of course, the plants become tall and bushy with 5-foot flower stems topped with flat heads of white flowers, of the cow parsley type. The scented suggestion of the name does not refer to the flowers, which are not strongly scented, but to the aromatic flavour of the leaves. These taste of horehound, and have delicate fragrance when dried. I was interested to see this plant growing very luxuriantly in Ann Hathaway's cottage garden in Stratford-on-Avon. As ground cover it needs plenty of room and fairly wild conditions, because the plants are quite buxom when full grown. The time to plant is when it is very young, because the long tap roots are very determined not to give way and it is difficult to move a big plant without breaking them. But there are usually plenty of seedlings round the parent plants and one or two plants will very soon produce enough small fry to cover large areas.

After the delicate cut leaves of corydalis and myrrhis the large shiny foliage of *Fatshedera* × *lizei* comes as a great contrast. This plant is a cross between *Fatsia japonica* and hedera (ivy) and has the best qualities of both parents. The leaves have the size of the fatsia and the beautiful glistening texture of the ivy. They seem to exude good health and sometimes take on pleasant shades of crimson and bronze in the autumn. I have been surprised at the way this plant has stood up to extremes of cold in recent winters. When nearly every plant above the snow line had become brown and desiccated the fatshedera remained completely unperturbed and was one of the few evergreens fit to cut. I always consider *Mahonia aquifolium* very tough and therefore useful for cutting in bad winters, but even that has succumbed to our recent winters; fatshedera, on the other hand, has remained unmoved. It makes a large informal plant, and I grow it tumbling down a shady bank in my ditch garden. The stems are lax, so if it is grown as a shrub or trained against a wall or fence it would need plenty of support. The flowers are the usual ones of the Irish ivy, *Hedera hibernica*, followed by black berries, and they are a pleasant addition to the winter scene, although it is not primarily for them that one grows the plant.

On a much more modest scale *Teucrium scordium crispum* offers another variety of interesting foliage. It has smallish leaves in soft grey-green, with a matt texture, and edges as tightly crimped and ruffled as the most curled variety of parsley. It grows close to the ground and does not spread very fast although it is easily propagated. The flowers are small and insignificant, in greenish-yellow, and grow on foot high stems. This is a plant I should use in rather prominent but not big areas which need cover that is interesting and attractive but which does not get out of hand.

~ 2 ~
Smother Plants

Not all ground cover plants are small and neat. The low-growing carpeters are best in some places, but in flower borders, narrow beds under hedges, and corners that can be completely filled with plants that grow luxuriantly, there are many plants that will suppress the weeds and provide flowers as well.

Nepeta faassenii is one of the best plants for the purpose, with its soft grey-green leaves and endless succession of lavender blue flowers. It flowers right through the season and needs only the removal of dead flowers underneath once or twice during the summer. It is a good subject for inaccessible places because it needs so little attention, and a normal plant will easily cover a square yard of soil. For positions where something really big can be used there is *N.* Six Hills Variety, which is a real giant and twice the size of *N. faassenii*.

Unquestionably *Phuopsis stylosa* smothers everything in sight. It has foliage that is among the brightest and freshest in the garden, and for most of the summer is covered with bright pink flowers, but it has a queer musky smell that not everyone likes. To me it has a suggestion of fox, other people seem to find it pleasanter, because I have seen it included in lists of scented plants. It makes enormous frothing mats about a foot high and roots as it goes. It also seeds itself quite satisfactorily, but some of the seedlings have rather washy flowers. The foliage gets rather out of hand by late autumn, and then I pull it out in handfuls, leaving enough to make a green film over the soil.

The broad leathery leaves of *Limonium latifolium*, which used to be called statice and is commonly known as 'sea lavender', cover quite a large area, and when the enormous sprays of tiny lavender flowers are out they make such a smother that they fill in the space between shrubs or tall perennials. The flowers dry beautifully and keep their colour, and have a delightful softening effect on bold dried arrangements, but if they can be left on the plant they will remain attractive until a wintry wind blows them to pieces. The stems are brittle, and though in normal conditions they will last until after Christmas, a few bad storms can spoil them.

In a normal year the dark reddish leaves of *Penstemon heterophyllus* look nice all through the winter, but a very hard frost can make them curl and become discoloured. This penstemon has a horizontal habit of growth and its long flat stems about a foot above ground will spread over several square feet of soil. The blue flowers have tinges of pink and after their main flowering in early summer come and go until late autumn. An excellent penstemon for the rock garden is *P. newberryi* which has pink flowers borne in profusion in July.

It comes as a surprise to find that *Dimorphotheca barberiae** is quite hardy. This South African plant is rather leafy for the number of soft pink, dark-eyed daisies it produces, but as a smother plant it is ideal. Even after a very hard winter the evergreen leaves will be quite unperturbed and still cover quite a lot of space. There is a more compact form of this daisy which has more flowers per square foot but not so much leafage, and is therefore not so good for ground cover. The bushy *D. ecklonis**, which has sparkling white flowers with blue centres, is definitely not hardy, although by the end of the season it has made a big bushy plant which covers about a square yard. The prostrate form of this white dimorphotheca seems to be much hardier except in unusually hard winters, and it makes a good carpet.

For a shady spot *Viola cornuta* spreads, smothers and flowers, and if there are convenient taller perennials nearby it likes to grow through them. I find the white-flowered form particularly robust and easy, and if one has time to keep the dead flowers cut it will go on producing flowers until very late autumn. I have never had as much success with the purple-headed form, but other people seem to be luckier.

Although the ordinary double feverfew is a wild plant I have always admired its occasional appearance in the garden and turned a blind eye to it when weeding. Now I can forget its plebeian background and make it welcome in the garden, for there is an improved cultivated form in *Chrysanthemum parthenium* White Bonnet*, which has the same fresh evergreen foliage and large white, green-eyed flowers. It grows rather exuberantly and needs keeping within bounds, otherwise the brittle stems may snap, with their weight of flower and leaf. Cuttings root very easily and a batch of small plants grown in an empty space will soon thicken to make a solid cover of brilliant green.

Though the individual stems of *Genista Lydia* are very slender, there are so many of them that nothing unwanted could raise its head where it is growing. When each stem is thickly covered with bright yellow flowers the effect is dazzling, almost too dazzling if the background is wrong. This genista needs a soothing setting; green, white or silver plants are best to show up the very strong colour. After this dazzling display is over the green stems remain pleasantly green and grow thickly enough to stop all weeds.

Between tall shrubs the pink cow parsley, *Pimpinella major*, is a good plant to use, for it is evergreen and makes thick clumps with pretty fern-like leaves. When the flowers are in bloom they come on 2 foot branching stems which are bushy enough to fill completely the space between shrubs. To be quite honest, the plant is not nearly as pretty as the ordinary white cow parsley of our hedgerows. But in spite of its delicate froth of flower and lovely foliage we do not often invite Queen Anne's Lace into our gardens, although the less pleasing pink form is made welcome in shrub borders and the wilder parts of the garden. The pink of the flowers is rather dull, I might almost say dirty, and has no sparkle of its own, but it is a good mixer and shows up the beauty of more colourful plants.

Another plant I grow between shrubs and which makes a very big clump by the autumn is a small red scabious, *Scabiosa rumelica*. Though the individual flowers are small there are a lot of them, and the clumps get very big by autumn. They need early staking and care has to be taken as they increase to give them adequate support that is not too noticeable. I use my rounded metal supports in rather light weight and try to put them in early. If left too late the clumps are reduced to market bunches if the supports are put in, but if the plants are staked early the mass of foliage, stem and flower will completely hide them and all one sees is a mass of pleasant vegetation filling a big space which could be uncomfortably bare or disgracefully weedy.

All the santolinas make big bushy plants in time and most of them are dwarf and informal in growth. The green-leaved form is particularly useful for covering the ground, either among stones or at the front of a border. *S. pinnata* is the one I grow because I prefer the lemon of its flowers to the rich gold of *S. virens* (*S. viridis*) which has real 'egg-yolk' flowers. Most of the silver-leaved santolinas have strong yellow flowers except for *sulphurea*, which is a form of *S. neapolitana* and has deep ivory flowers instead of yellow ones, but the foliage is not as silvery as the ordinary form. *S.* Lemon Queen is another with slightly greener foliage and flowers nearer ivory than gamboge.

For a real smother plant *S. neapolitana* is the best to choose for the mass of its delicate, very silver filigree foliage. *S. serratifolia* is more bushy and more spreading in growth, while *S. chamaecyparissus* (*incana*) is the neatest of all with tight silver leaves. *S. c. compacta* is a smaller, more compact form which is rather too controlled for covering much ground.

All the santolinas do best if trimmed to the ground each spring, but that is something I find difficult to do because the foliage is useful for decoration as well as for cuttings and I hate to waste it, but it is a silly point of view, because if one delays too long the plants get out of hand and become leggy and untidy.

In a normal year *Ballota pseudodictamnus* keeps its normal happy demeanour throughout the winter and its soft grey-green leaves are very pleasant in the cold weather. But in a very bad spell of cold and frosty weather it can look a little discouraged. But that is the exception rather than the rule and I would recommend it as a good plant to grow where something rather free and shrubby is needed to fill a space, especially if fairly young plants are used. It is the old woody ones that die in winter. I used to think that this plant was a small phlomis, and its leaves have the same soft furry texture. But its flowering habits are different. It makes 2-foot stems studded all their length with downy calyces, in which nestle small mauve-pink flowers. They are pretty when they first come out, but get untidy after a week or so, and I always enjoy my plants better when I can trim off the flower stems and depend for enjoyment on the mounds of small soft leaves.

For a hot dry spot where something dwarf and spreading is needed to keep down weeds and make a pleasing colour scheme all through the summer *Dorycnium hirsutum** is a possibility. The small pointed leaves are silver-grey, with a silky surface, with many small pink and white pea-like flowers, which are followed by shiny black seed pods. It is hardy except in unusually cold weather.

Helianthemums also like to be baked, and they make large spreading mats and being evergreen are particularly useful. Some of them have silver leaves, others dark glossy green, and some grey-green. Flowers, of course, can be double or single in any shade of pink, crimson or orange, with some yellow and white, and the plants can be very low growing or more upright. All of them need drastic trimming after flowering and if, after a few years, there are dead stems under the top growth they should be cut out.

Though it can be almost a pest the little rock erigeron, *E. mucronatus**, can fill up many a bare space with endless clouds of white and pink daisies. It is wisest not to plant it where it can be a menace to more valuable plants, for it seeds and burrows and is no respecter of its betters, but where it can increase as much as it wants it is a most useful collaborator, flowering right into early winter. It is not evergreen but the thick mass of brittle dark stems are not unattractive in the winter and need not be cut down until the spring, when it will start to do it all over again.

Though *Gypsophila repens* is not so pushing and keeps itself to itself, it makes a good cover about 2 feet square and in June and July its showers of airy white or pink flowers add lightness among darker plants. And when the flowers are over the tousled stems are quite attractive for some weeks longer.

For most of the year Lady's Mantle, *Alchemilla mollis*, has more than a little to offer. Its leaves are among the most beautiful I know, as neatly pleated as a fan and greyish-green in colour. Their surface is somewhat downy, which emphasises the soft colouring. The flowers are tiny stars in very pale green and borne in feathery sprays about 18 inches high. They are lovely at all times, as they begin to open from their enveloping leaves, and when they fill a wide space with shimmering clouds of green. It is a temptation to cut many of the stems, for nothing is so good with every kind of flower, and many gardeners advise the cutting of the heads before they have time to seed, but I have never enough of these entrancing plants and every little downy seedling is welcome. The leaves die down in winter but do not disappear completely, and the clumps are so thick and matted that no weeds grow near them.

A. alpine is a much more delicate plant; everything is on a smaller scale and it is best in smaller patches where the small leaves, margined with silver and lined with silver satin, can be appreciated. The flowers are a very pale silvery-green and come in 6-inch sprays. It spreads enough to make a good cover, but it does not make impenetrable clumps like *A. mollis*.

One of the most successful and beautiful smother plants I know is *Geranium wallichianum* Buxton's Blue*. It is surprising what an enormous clump of leafy stems grow from a single crown, and in gardens where there are odd corners that need filling and gaps between shrubs which ask for a smother of leaf and flower there is nothing better than this geranium. The leaves are well cut and well marked with different shades of green. They take on many tones of amber and crimson in the autumn, when the flowers are at their peak, and make a perfect setting for the powder blue flowers, which open wide to show the central patch of white. There is another geranium which grows in the same way but has bright pink instead of blue flowers. *G. grevilleanum** is not often seen, and though it has not the serene look of *G.* Buxton's Blue it is quite pretty grown in the same way.

Another geranium that grows into a frothing mass, spangled with salmon-pink flowers, is *g. endressii* Wargrave*. It grows taller than the normal *G. endressii*, which is mat forming, and is ideal for bridging the gap between shrubs. I grow it between *Chamaecyparis lawsoniana fletcheri** and elaeagnus and it completely fills the space and is absolutely weed-proof.

A hardy fuchsia that I find makes a splendid mound of arching stems from a solid mass of hard stems is Mrs Popple. One plant will account for a good square yard and several together would fill the space with bright foliage and showy crimson and purple flowers. Nothing would have a chance to grow beneath this close canopy which retains something of its shape if the stems are left on during the winter and cut down in spring. The small hardy *F.* Tom Thumb will do the same thing on a smaller scale. It is a foot high and covers a square foot of soil. Some people find the crimson and white Mme Cornelissen quite hardy and I have seen this grown in the same way. But in many districts I think one would be advised to protect the plants in autumn with ashes and bracken.

If *Indigofera gerardiana* (*floribunda*) were completely hardy it would make a very good smother plant, because it grows from the base every year and flowers freely. With its light grey-green foliage and purple pea-like flowers it is extremely pretty against silver or variegated shrubs. It can be cut back hard in April, and will make a bushy plant in mild districts, growing up to 4 feet with a spread of 6 to 9 feet. It will grow in shade quite well, and if one lives in one of the warmer parts of the country it is a plant worth considering.

~ 3 ~
Herbaceous Ground Cover

How often one reads a reference about a herbaceous plant 'makes good ground cover'; there are many plants that, although usually thought of purely as herbaceous plants, can also be used to cover ground attractively, ground which otherwise might be unsightly with weeds, or merely bare.

To many people the idea of ground cover is something very neat and ground-hugging but actually anything that covers the ground with a growing carpet of green can be classed as ground cover. In some places the taller plants are more in keeping.

Sometimes it is in summer particularly that the ground cover is needed and in such places one of the deciduous plants is quite suitable, but in situations that are in permanent observation, such as courtyards, ground next to buildings and conspicuous corners, evergreen plants that are endued with perpetual youth are wanted.

One of the best of these is *Euphorbia robbiae**. When I mention the places where I have seen it growing it will be quite clear what I mean. I first noticed it in Miss Nellie Britton's garden near Tiverton where it was growing under a hedge in the far end of the garden. This was a part of a singularly interesting and well kept garden that could easily have been almost squalid. A hedge on one side, a tree on the other, a chicken run below and not many of the interesting plants that were everywhere else in the garden, it was not a place in which to linger. But *E. robbiae* saved the situation. Miss Britton was a very great gardener and she knew the right plant for every place. Here the euphorbia hid the untidy hedge and suppressed the various weeds the hedge encouraged. It filled the space between hedge and path with foot-high stems of tufted foliage. The leaves of this spurge are dull surfaced like many others but a much darker green. The rounded leaves grow in whorls up the stems and above come the flowers. In January there will be hanging buds (it is a family trait of the euphorbias to bend over the tops of the flower stems while the buds are swelling and then to straighten out afterwards). They open early in the year to green flowers with flat green bracts, and those flowers hang on somehow through to the dark days of winter. How it is done I do not know but I am sure that the drying, dying flowers I cut off in December are those I watched opening in January.

Visitors to Oxford may have seen this euphorbia making a green bank against the old buildings of Magdalen College, and in the Oxford Botanic Garden opposite, *E. robbiae* fills corners at the bottom of the buildings at the entrance to the gardens. In my own garden I planted it at the edge of a path crossing the ditch and leading to a grassy strip. The euphorbia has made a miniature forest outlining the path and filling a space between it and a pollarded willow. This euphorbia runs in a ladylike way and it also seeds itself mildly which makes it an even more valuable ground cover plant.

Hellebores also have very dark foliage but I will not pretend it is quite as good as *E. robbiae*, because it gets rather dog-eared and shabby by the end of the year and is sometimes unworthy of the lovely flowers that open from November onwards. But if the leaves can be inferior the flowers are vastly superior and among the most ravishing blooms of the winter. Like the euphorbia, hellebores do best in shade and can be used to fill in any space in shade with reasonably good soil. I use them under north walls, under trees and in shady beds. Shrub roses grow more popular and among the various plants chosen to grow with them hellebores are high on the list. The hellebores would appreciate the good living accorded to the roses and the peaceful life they get among the roses which are as permanent as themselves.

Practically all hellebores make good ground cover except the few deciduous ones, *Helleborus viridis, intermedia (torquatus), cyclophyllus* and *purpurascens*. *H. atrorubens* is not as leafy as some for the plum-coloured flowers often appear in November without leaves and have a bare time till the leaves come along in the spring.

One of the best ground cover hellebores is *H. foetidus*. it is one of our native plants and has beautifully cut very dark foliage contrasting with the flowering sprays which have palest green flowers, stems and leaves. This is not a very long-lived plant but it seeds itself well.

We have always called the Corsican hellebore *H. corsicus* but its other name *H. argutifolius* seems to be gaining ground and is no doubt more correct. This hellebore is sometimes planted in less shady places as it is not so insistent on shade as the others. No other hellebore has the pale grey-green netted leaves, toothed like holly, or is furnished early in life with great clusters of apple green flowers. Often flowering the second year, by the end of a few years this hellebore may be tall and need support. It should never be planted in a windy place if proper support is not provided because its stems are too heavily laden for wind.

One gets to know which of the lenten roses (the *H. orientalis* type) have the best leaves. I would put *H. kochii* high on the list. It is an early-flowering variety and fresh green foliage accompanies the wide cream flowers. Some of the plum-purples such as *H.* Apotheker Bogren and *H. abchasicus* have very large dark leaves, sometimes tinged with violet. The pink-flowered *H.* Aurora and *H.* Apple Blossom and the greeny white *H. olympicus* all have medium rather fresh green leaves.

It is strange that one never hears about the foliage of the Christmas rose, *H. niger*, only its flowers and whether they come early and have long stalks, are pure white or pink flushed, grow above or below the leaves singly on their stems or in pairs. The leaves of this hellbore are very dark and neatly shaped and they do not get blown about as a rule. They make marvellous permanent plantings in any shady place, needing reasonably good soil, moisture in dry weather and an occasional mulch. The most outstanding Christmas rose of recent years is of course the very large pure white, *H.* Potter's Wheel.

*Acanthus mollis latifolius** has most beautiful leaves, large and glossy and normally quite evergreen in my part of the country (Somerset) but not always so good in a very hard winter. The plants are quite hardy and will always reappear in all their glory even after a beating in the winter, though recent winters have taught us they are not the tough evergreens we thought they were.

Like many plants that are hard to eradicate acanthus is extremely slow to establish, and it is not easy to get up pieces with good roots. I do not know how far down the roots go because I have never got to the bottom of them but I do know that once in the garden they can never be ousted. I made the mistake of planting one in the middle of a border and though I chop away all the time it reappears each year and seems to get more, not less.

But where it can be left to increase it provides most handsome leaves and flower spikes and each bit will soon cover about a square yard of soil. *A. mollis* has the larger leaves; they are bright green and very glossy, and arch above tall stems. The edges are lobed but not spiny.

I think *A. spinosus* is more often seen than *A. mollis*, it being a smaller neater plant and more suitable for normal gardens, while *A. mollis* needs a large scene. The leaves of *spinosus* are very dark green, more deeply cut, with spiny points. They are about half the size of *A. mollis*.

The flowers of the spiny acanthus are vicious to handle because each hooded mauve flower has a spiny leaf beneath it. These flowers grow on spikes 4 to 5 feet long and are most impressive growing, and equally good as cut flowers. They dry well, for their papery pale mauve flowers with grey-green hoods and leaves mix with anything, and are the making of a massive arrangement. Large, soft, downy leaves used as cover between small-leaved shrubs make happy contrast. The leaves of *Salvia sclarea turkestanica* have violet stems and violet veins on their grey-green surfaces, and make very large handsome rosettes which are lovely for winter enjoyment. A good rosette will cover about 2 ft. sq. and if three are planted together a good area of bare earth can be crossed off. Of course this salvia has handsome spikes of flower in summer, palest blue with lilac bracts, and is a biennial, usually producing enough seedlings to carry on.

The leaves of foxgloves are also good even before the flowers occur, and those of symphytum very long and graceful. Some of the symphytums are frankly too coarse and invasive for any but very wild places in the garden. They seed themselves and becoming embarrassingly big. In the Oxford Botanic Garden the white-flowered *S. tauricum* has been allowed its head in a large shady bed and is a wonderful sight with its white flowers and rather pale green foliage. I was warned not to give it a good position in my garden; I did not need to give, it helped itself to a chunk of the rock garden and I dig up seedlings every year. But one of the plants here has become completely variegated so the brute has won so far as that specimen is concerned.

There is another variegated symphytum, *S. × uplandicum variegatum*, which does well in a shaded place but it does not increase enough to make good ground cover. *S. caucasicum* increases very well and is so unfussy about soil that it is a good plant to use in poor soil under trees. Its leaves are not so big as some, and are long and narrow in grey-green with a suggestion of blue, and go well with the deep gentian-blue flowers. It increases and it seeds, so it is a very good plant for quick co-operation. The comfrey, *S. officinale* can have flowers of blue, mauve, pink or crimson, but *S. peregrinum*, which has pale blue tubular flowers on arching stems, is rather taller. Its buds are often pink and it is a splendid plant in a place where a hairy, coarse, large-leaved plant can be used.

S. grandiflorum is the best of all the symphytums for ground cover but the least spectacular. It is more dwarf than the others with very dark, hairy leaves, and increases by long stems, which root at their tips, rather like *Omphalodes verna* on a bigger scale. It soon covers any place in which it is introduced but it is easily curtailed, as the branching stems can be pulled out in handfuls. It flowers very early in the year and has orange-tipped cream bells, which are quite attractive when they open in the early spring but would not get much attention later in the year.

Trachystemon orientalis can be put almost in the same class. It is a very coarse plant that will grow anywhere, however bad the soil, and has large hairy leaves which smother everything in sight. The blue flowers are small but very attractive and they appear in early spring before the leaves get too robust.

I expect I shall be rebuked for mentioning *Brunnera macrophylla* in the next breath for in many gardens it is quite a refined plant and does not get overpowering. I enjoy it in early spring when the hairy heart-shaped leaves are a good green and not too big. Then the dainty sprays of forget-me-not blue flowers are in proportion to the plant and one enjoys the compact clumps covering the ground under trees, in soil that is not too dry. It is an excellent plant for covering shady ground, but it gets big and coarse later in the year, the big leaves get shabby, and though the brave little flowers continue to open one needs to remove all the old leaves if they are to have a showing. It seeds well and if I had time to dig up the seedlings for a cover of fresh young plants instead of old ones I would like it better.

There may be several herbaceous phlomis but I know one only and that sometimes appears under the name of *P. samia* but is more correctly called *P. viscosa* or *P. russelliana*. It is a most satisfactory plant because it is always the same and can be used in any conspicuous position where good foliage is needed. It makes very flat rosettes of large wrinkled hoary leaves, which are larger and more heart-shaped near the base. It spreads, but quite neatly, and is very easy to propagate because it breaks up into these numerous rosettes. I grow it near the front of a raised bed, and it is quickly edging over the stones. The flowers are typical whorls in primrose, with the stems growing up through them, so that at the end they are about 4 feet tall with the flowers at intervals. The flowers come late, so I choose early-flowering companions and often leave on the old stems as winter garnish.

*Geranium ibericum** has dark hairy leaves, but they grow on foot high stems and look best in a mass a short way into a bed rather than right under one's eye. I used this geranium, or rather its better variety *G. i. platypetalum**, under *Magnolia grandiflora* Exmouth, an early-flowering form which can be grown in the open. The geranium has made a sea of tossing dark leaves under the richness of bronze and glistening green, and is a lovely sight when covered with large violet-purple flowers in June. It makes a very close root system so no intruders can push through to spoil the spectacle.

Two other geraniums with good leaves also have the same dense root systems, both have good angular leaves on 18 inch stems, and tiny hovering flowers with reflexed petals, in shades of mauve and purple. One, *G. reflexum*, has plain leaves, and rather mauve-pink flowers, and the other is called *G. punctatum** because there is a maroon spot on each of the five lobes of the leaves. This variety has deeper purplish petals reflexed from a maroon point. Sometimes the leaves of *G. punctatum** are almost primrose coloured in the spring, and then the spots show up very well. The leaves also turn in autumn, so it is a good plant for bringing interesting colour to the scene, and seems to grow well in sun as well as shade.

The grey-green crinkled leaves of *G. renardii* are beautiful against red-leaved shrubs, or even with silver if a cool refined scheme is fancied. I have heard this

9-inch geranium called dull, but I think it depends where it is grown. It is not showy and the greyish-white flowers do not dazzle, but they are delicately pencilled with violet-purple and worth a long look. They show up best when the plants are not too big, and so it pays to divide them quite often. I find this geranium will grow in sun or shade.

And so will *G. macrorrhizum*. Although it often sows itself in shade in my garden, in sun it makes a much more dwarf plant, its leaves turn better in autumn, and it becomes a close carpet of well-shaped aromatic leaves.

There are four different coloured varieties of this geranium. The type has magenta-pink flowers, which are prettier than they sound, and in *G. m. roseum* the flowers are pink. I have as well, a form labelled Ingwersen's Variety which is rather bigger. It grows to about 15 inches instead of 12, and has larger flowers. For ordinary ground I prefer the low-growing common form but if the plant is to be part of a colour scheme in a border Ingwersen's Var. is undoubtedly the one to choose. My favourite for all purposes is *G. m. album**, which has red stems and red calyces to the white flowers. I may be imagining it but I always feel that this one is the most dwarf, and I am sure it colours best. *G. macrorrhizum* increases in rather an angular way. It does not make the thick clumps of *G. ibericum** and others of that type nor does it delve below the surface like the bloody crane's bill. It has adventuring stems which root in time but very often explore some way before doing so, and they are brittle. It is easy to break off pieces, plant them and wait for them to root, but to take off rooted pieces needs more care.

I have seen suggestions that *Centaurea dealbata* makes good ground cover. It certainly makes good clumps of grey-green leaves, lined with silver, from 18 inches to 2 feet high. I know I have great trouble to keep this plant from bursting from my restraining bonds and I can imagine three or five clumps would fill the space between shrubs or large perennials with a thicket of light leaves, with relays of pink sweet sultan flowers from June to October.

But I have never seen it proposed that *C. montana* could be used for the same purpose. Yet it seems to me it is a 'natural' for the job. Half the neglected vicarage gardens in the country are full of its silver leaves and shaggy cornflower heads mostly in blue, but sometimes in white or pink and if there were places in the garden that needed covering it would, I am sure, be happy to oblige. Ever since I have had a garden I have been curtailing a big clump of the blue-flowered form of this centaurea, which was given to me from our vicarage garden when I first came to the village. I always wish the pink- and white-flowered forms were as persistent. I grow these two as ground cover under a crab apple and I never have to be as brutal to them as I am to the vicarage brand, and even that is far more attractive than bare earth or weeds.

Also very bright green and glossy, the foliage of doronicum is good at all times of year, always looking fresh and full of good health. The plants increase quite quickly and make solid fleshy lumps, with their succession of bright golden daisies from April till June. There are several new doronicums but I still think the old stager, *D.* Harpur Crewe* is as good as any.

Polemoniums have neat foliage and those which go on flowering over a long period make good subjects to use with bigger plants. One of the best for thickening up to fill empty spaces is *P.* Lambrook Mauve, which makes a big shaggy clump and has relays of lilac flowers until late November. It does not run but is very easily increased by division.

Plants that make a smother of stems, flowers and foliage during the summer fill the spaces in the border and give it a fully-clothed look. My first acquaintance with *Erodium manescavi* was in a friend's garden when I saw the plants in early spring looking like large green starfishes laid out on the soil. The leaves are good, grey-green and hairy, and about a foot long. When the plant starts to flower in June it goes on until late autumn; in fact there are buds waiting to open when winter stops its season. To get plenty of flowers a rather poor soil is best. On a rich diet there will be such luxuriant foliage that the flowers will be swamped. This plant is interesting in all its stages and is usually a tangle of buds, magenta-pink flowers and green seed-heads which look like the head and beak of a heron. For just as *geranos*, a crane, gives us the name of geranium, crane's bill, so *pelargos*, s stork, is the source of pelargonium and *erodius*, a heron, is the source of erodium. All the same I have never heard pelargoniums called stork's bills or erodiums heron's bills, but I believe these names were in common use before the sixteenth century.

Anyone who grows the old-fashioned day-lily, *Hemerocallis fulva fl. pl.*, knows how it increases and fills up all the space available. Half a dozen shoots soon become fifty and when the plant is in full leaf a good clump can easily cover more than a square yard. Day-lilies, ferns and bulbs make a shady border that will take care of itself and present a decent appearance at all times.

Many of the herbaceous plants that lose their leaves make such solid root structure that no weeds can get through and when we cut down the old stems the ground cover becomes underground cover. *Lysimachia clethroides* is a conscientious worker and will fill in its appointed space with solid ranks of 2-foot leafy stems, each topped with a spike of white flowers bent like a shepherd's crook. There will be flowers from July to September and even then the finished heads are not unattractive. The leaves of this loosestrife turn to lovely shades of crimson and russet in the autumn, and even when they brown with age I find it hard to part with them. When wild wintry winds make them too untidy they have to be cut down to a red-brown stubble and then one is grateful for the tangle of bright pink roots below. For from each stem there radiate a dozen or more fleshy roots, which are really underground stems with a shoot at the end of each all ready to pop up to the surface and become a new plant. *L. punctata* has fleshy roots too, and they also are underground stems which surface where they can, but this plant runs whereas the other merely radiates. If there is an empty space near a pond that wants attractive cover *L. punctata* could well be introduced. It has typical creeping jenny flowers in whorls up the stems, interspersed with bright green leaves (its other name is *L. verticillata*) and is a plant that can be enjoyed when it has room to spread without swamping other people. There is a form called *L. p. ocelata* in which each flower has a deep orange eye. The wild yellow loosestrife, *L. vulgaris*, is quite pretty for naturalising, with its loose sprays of flowers.

Though thalictrum does not run but keeps itself to itself the clumps soon become large and solid and several planted fairly close together among shrubs give pleasure for a very long time. Among big shrubs I have seen the tall *speciosissimum* (*glaucum*) used most effectively. The large clumps of blue maidenhair leaves are lovely and make fine colour contrast, and later fluffy heads of lemon flowers are pretty against dark foliage, *T. aquilegiifolium* grows to about 1½ to 2 feet only and when the heads of mauve or cream are over there remain mounds of beautiful grey-green foliage, like that of a columbine. *T. minus* (*T. majus* or *adiantifolium*) makes a thicket of fern-like foliage, with greenish flowers and can become rather invasive.

*Dracocephalum prattii** is not evergreen but it is such a willing worker that it is worth considering when bold treatment for wide areas is needed. It has thick penetrating roots and makes good use of them, so much so that I plant it in a large drain pipe when it is included in a border. But among shrubs where its grey-green leaves and soft blue flowers can be allowed to wander it makes a pleasant indistinct plant, not unlike a giant creeping catmint.

*Amsonia salicifolia** is not orthodox ground cover either, but it is very effective. There are strong differences of opinion about the name of this plant, and neither side will give way. I was given my plant by a very great gardener and I stick to the name I was given then, but many people know it as *Rhazya orientalis* and it appears like that in some catalogues. Actually there are two very similar plants. Mine is American and rhazya comes from Asia. I would call it a 'filling in' plant, because it makes a veritable thicket of 18-inch stems set with narrow grey-green leaves, with flat heads of tiny starry flowers in soft, slaty blue – I grow it between a large crimson peony and a tall pink rose and it fills in the space so easily that I never have to worry about it at all. It has tough underground stems shaggy with fibrous roots, which run and divide throwing up fresh stems as they go. The flowers last for many weeks and are that gentle shade of blue that is so complimentary to the reds, pinks and even magentas of the flower world.

~ 4 ~
Cover for Woodland

The damp shady soil under trees can easily become overgrown and swamped with weeds, yet it is also very easy to find attractive plants that will make a pleasing carpet. One of the humblest and yet most efficient is *Lysimachia nummularia*, our modest little Creeping Jenny. It is often found in rather damp places although it does not insist on a very moist position, but it does enjoy shade. Though I am quite attached to the plant, with bright lacquered leaves and large golden flowers which creep about, supposedly demanding damp soil but quite happy anywhere, it is invasive, and once it gets into a garden will appear in most unexpected places. I try to discourage the ordinary Creeping Jenny because I have quite enough to do to keep the golden variety in its place. This is a gay little plant and brings sunshine in its wake. I want it to make bands of gold at the sides of the stones at the bottom of my ditch garden, but it swarms up over the stones that hold up the bank, carpets one pocket after another, and would festoon both sides of the ditch if I would let it. It is a wonderful plant for dark corners.

Mitella breweri is neater than the lysimachia but it is nearly as persistent. I try to keep it for making a green cover on the steep banks between the pockets of the ditch, pockets in which I grow special primroses, trilliums and aroids, and it spends its life trying to leave the slippery slope for a pleasant horizontal life in good soil in the pockets. It has neat very flat leaves and works its way over the soil making quite a thick and fibrous cover. The flowers are inconspicuous unless one takes a magnifying glass to admire the delicacy of those short sprays of tiny green flowers.

Quite a number of ground cover plants will grow happily in either sun or shade, but there are some plants that must be grown in shade. The barrenworts, epimediums, are particularly good shade plants for ground cover. They have tough nobbly roots which are so congested that weeds cannot penetrate them and their foliage is mostly evergreen and lovely throughout the year. It is particularly delightful in the spring when the delicate green is dappled with warm shades of brown mahogany, and in the autumn when it turns bronze and crimson. Very often the leaves are cut off just before flowering time to give the flowers a chance, but not all experts agree with this. In low-lying districts the flowers are subject to frost damage if they have not the protection of their leaves.

When I first saw *Rubus fockeanus* it was growing on acid soil, and I planted mine in the peat garden where it does extremely well. Whether it will grow as well in my limy soil I mean to find out one day, because it would be an admirable cover for the pockets in which I grow species snowdrops. It is absolutely prostrate and its neat trails work stealthily over the soil, rooting as they grow. It does flower, but so unobtrusively that the small greenish flowers can easily be overlooked. They are almost hidden by the dull green crinkled leaves.

Also rather flat, that old cottage plant, *Saxifraga stolonifera* (*S. sarmentosa*), the much loved Mother of Thousands, spreads quite quickly; it has most beautiful leaves which colour well. Because it is usually seen growing in pots in cottage windows there is an idea that it is not quite hardy, but I know it in several gardens which cannot be called balmy and it seems perfectly happy, and when we think of all the little plants that appear on the ends of its numerous runners it is obvious that it is ground cover *par excellence*.

The mouse plant, *Arisarum proboscideum*, is rather a rarity for many of us, but give it a damp shady site and leave it alone and it will spread in all directions. In the late A. T. Johnson's lovely garden in the Conway Valley this little plant has multiplied so that now there are large carpets of it, and the small glistening arum leaves break into waves as they sway in the wind. I visited the garden in August and I thought how fascinating would be the sight in spring when the leaves would be nearer the ground and the long brown spathes of the small arum flowers visible like so many long tails of mice disappearing down their holes.

Some gardeners may be shocked to see our little native woodruff, *Asperula odorata**, as a cultivated plant in the garden, but I think it is as pretty as many garden plants and I have deliberately introduced and encouraged it to carpet some of my shady slopes. It is not evergreen but the dark tufted stems of narrow leaves reappear each year to be followed by fragrant white flowers.

The feathery foliage of the baneberries is attractive for the greater part of the year. *Actaea rubra* is the species most usually grown, and it has red berries in tall spikes after small white flowers – *A. spicata* is a rare native, which has black berries after small white flowers. The most striking is *A. s. alba**, which has white berries on red stems after its small white flowers. Although the actaeas do not run they make solid clumps with spreading foliage, and have a root formation rather like that of a spiraea. They grow very easily from seed or can be divided.

It is not only what *Eomecon chionanthum* does above ground that makes it a good ground cover plant, but one has also to consider the mass of running roots below the surface. To look at the leaves and the almost transparent stems no one would think that the Poppy of the Dawn had such determination, but explore with a fork and there are strong fleshy roots going in all directions. This plant is a distant relation of 'bloodrot' (*Sanguinaria Canadensis*) and has the same strange red sap, and there is a distinct resemblance in the shape of the leaves and the texture of the stems. But I have never found that bloodroot runs, and that is one thing eomecon does with great ease. I wish it would flower as readily, and I feel sure if we could curtail its underground activities somehow it would flower better. The flowers are small and like a white miniature poppy in form, with yellow stamens. It likes a cool shady spot that is not too dry, but grows just as well in limy as in lime-free soil.

With such big fleshy roots a colony of solomon's seal (*Polygonatum multiflorum*) makes good ground cover, particularly our native plant which varies between 1 and 2 feet. The hanging, white, green-tipped flowers are waisted in the middle, have no scent, and turn to blue-black berries. More rare the angular solomon's seal, *P. odoratum* (*P. officinale*), has larger flowers which are scented and unwaisted. The stems are angled and it is usually shorter than the ordinary solomon's seal. The whorled solomon's seal, *P. verticillatum*, has very strong swollen creeping rootstocks, so makes a good protection against weeds. The stems vary from 1 to 3 feet and have many leaves in whorls, with two to three small white flowers at each whorl. The flowers are green tipped and unscented, and turn to small red berries. *P. oppositifolium* has small white star-like flowers at the top of 15-inch stems, and makes a good thicket of foliage.

Lilies-of-the-valley, *Convallaria majalis*, always seem to me to be ground cover for more sophisticated places than a woodland garden, but this plant can be planted under trees as well as under high walls, and soon thickens into a carpet of wide-ribbed leaves, and the hanging white bells become bright red berries.

Liriope graminifolia is another little grassy plant that will get bigger in a quiet way and can be easily increased by division. Sometimes called *L. muscari* or even *Ophiopogon spicatus*, it is often planted in sun and associated with nerines because it flowers at the same time, but I find the plants I grow in shade far happier than those in sun, and the stiff dark violet spikes more numerous.

Hostas make wonderful cover all through the summer, but their leaves die off in autumn and do not reappear until late spring. The large-leaved types make wonderful ground cover in shady places, at the borders of shrubberies and by the water-side in contrast to *Iris sibirica* or *Cyperus longus*. For ground cover the varieties with the biggest leaves are the best to choose, and the leaves are bigger when the plants are grown in shade. Hostas grown in the open are more compact and flower better, so for big leaves and luxuriant growth they should be confined to shade in soil that is occasionally enriched with manure and not allowed to get dry. In limy soils as much humus as possible should be given. The varieties with variegated or margined leaves are pretty in dark places, but they do not cover so much space as some of the others. The leaves of *H. crispula*, *H.* Thomas Hogg and *H. albomarginata* are margined with white in varying degrees, *H. undulata* and *H.*

u. media pieta have much creamy-white with the shining green of their leaves, and in *H. fortunei albopicta* the leaves unfurl a bright fresh yellow, which is the embodiment of spring, and have a border of pale green. Another form has leaves in pale yellow without a green border and in both cases the yellow turns primrose before the leaves are soft green all over.

For very big green leaves I would choose *H. ventricosa*, which has very large heart-shaped leaves of rather dark green. It is sometimes called *H. coerulea* or *H. latifolia* and has dark violet flowers.

In *H. sieboldiana* the leaves are also heart-shaped but glaucous; they are so deeply veined that they have a crinkled effect; it is sometimes called *H. glauca* or *H. fortunei robusta*. The flowers are rather pale lilac, but more than any of the others they hang on to their opened seedcases after the seeds have fallen and make attractive skeletons which last all through the winter.

In good, rather damp soil the tiarellas, particularly *T. cordifolia*, will grow quite fast and have good evergreen leaves. Astrantias too are evergreen and grow luxuriously in shade and fairly good soil. *A. major* does not run, but the clumps increase quite quickly and it seeds about, so it is a good woodland plant, and flowers from May to December. The creeping *A. maxima* (*A. helleborifolia**) is not evergreen and flowers once only, but its pink and green flowers are very pretty.

Some of the larger, less fussy plants can be used in a large garden, teasels and *Aruncus sylvester** (*Spiraea aruncus*), and the soft lavender *Lactuca* (*Mulgedium*) *bourgaei*, which has good foliage but seeds itself too liberally. Japanese anemones will increase and keep out weeds, and so will the cottage peonies, *Paeonia officinalis*, particularly the form with double crimson flowers, and as it makes enormous clumps with too many leaves for the flowers, it need not look like an escape from the garden.

Myrrhis odorata seeds too much for most places, but its feathery foliage and dainty cream flowers will cover a wide area, and the blue-green leaves of *Thermopsis montana*, with its golden laburnum-like flowers, would be welcome in the wilder parts of the garden. It runs very freely and has tough roots, so it prevents weeds and so does *Physalis franchetii*, with its orange lanterns in autumn, and although it is deciduous it has such a tough root system that it makes an underground carpet.

The bigger geraniums and the woodland euphorbias – *amygdaloides* and *hyberna* – all cover the ground and give pleasant foliage, even *Saponaria officinalis*, which is one of the worst creeping plants there is, albeit a pretty one, will make such thickets of foot high stems that nothing else will be able to get a foothold.

~ 5 ~

Carpeters

Carpeting plants such as are used in paving are often needed for filling spaces at sides of stone paths or in flat areas of the garden that are too small for grass and need a growing cover.

The creeping thymes are usually grown in full sun, but they will also grow in shade and do not take long to make a solid mat of aromatic foliage, and in June and July, when most of them flower, they become carpets of colour. The various forms of *Thymus serpyllum* make close carpets, for they have small leaves. Each plant will eventually spread to cover an area 15 or 18 inches square, and small plants should be planted 15 inches apart, but if a quicker cover is required they can be planted closer.

They range in colour from crimson to white. *T. s. coccineus* is the deepest in colour, with flowers of beetroot red, made richer by dark leaves. *T. s. c. majus* has the same colouring but is larger in every way. *T. s.* Russettings is a good deep pink, and then there are the soft tones of *T. s. roseus*. You can tell *T. s.* Annie Hall, whether it is in flower or not, because the leaves, which are particularly small and close, are a light green, a good background for the pale pink flowers. *T. s.* Pink Chintz is well named, the flowers are shell-pink and the leaves grey-green. With me the white flowers of *T. s. albus* are the last to open and I always look forward to their advent. The woolly grey leaves of *T. s. lanuginosus* come on long stems and have pink flowers. Another thyme with greyish leaves is *T. hirsutus doerfleri*. It is very dwarf and close growing and its small pink flowers are earlier than some. *T. herba-barona* comes from Corsica and gets its name from the fact that it was used in the cooking of barons of beef. It smells strongly of caraway, in fact I have been working near it in the middle of winter and have been made aware of its presence by the strong and delicious scent of caraway on the air.

Another plant with aromatic foliage that makes solid mats of bright green foliage is pennyroyal, *Mentha pulegium*. There are two forms of pennyroyal, the upright and the creeping, and it is the latter that makes the best carpeting plant. I like it best before it flowers, for the lavender flowers grow in whorls on stems about 8 or 9 inches high and soon look untidy, so that it is a relief when one can cut them off. There are other creeping mints. *M. gattefossei* has small pointed leaves and white flowers and increases by attaching its rather thick stems to the ground with penetrating white roots. The tiniest mint is *M. requienii*, and that also comes from Corsica. The leaves are microscopic and one needs a magnifying glass to enjoy the flowers, which are lavender. For all its fragility it has great determination and once in the garden will manage to keep a foothold somewhere, even on the top of a stone if it has been ousted from its stronghold in a flower-bed, and the tiniest scraps will grow if planted in good soil with sand and peat. One year it left the bed where it was growing and decided it liked the lawn better, and for several years it made a close carpet among the grass, from which I could help myself whenever I needed any. A very cold winter killed all that was growing in the grass, although not the plantings in beds and paving.

Camomile has very fine ferny leaves, and to step on a well-grown planting is like walking on a cushion. The double-flowered form, *Anthemis nobilis fl. pl.**, is the most attractive one to grow, and this or the single flowered variety is used for making chamomile lawns. The leaves are a particularly good bright green and they smell deliciously of apples if pressed by hand or foot.

It is necessary only to see how the mossy saxifrages spread in the rock garden to realise how useful they are for covering the soil. They do best in shade, but sun does not deter them. I grow between paving stones in my front garden a pale pink saxifrage I bought as Apple Blossom many years ago, but it does not appear in modern lists. It increases very fast and is often used as a border at the edge of flower beds. In the National Trust garden, Tintinhull, it borders a long bed of irises, many of them in shades of blue, and the colour association is very good.

In my garden it spreads in all directions, covering stone as easily as it does the soil of flower beds. I put it between the stones that border other flower beds and if I did not remove it by the basketful it would cover everything in sight.

There are a large number of mossy saxifrages and any of them can be used as ground cover. For quick results obtain *Saxifraga* James Bremner, which has large white flowers on 6-inch stalks and foliage in proportion. *S.* Elf is a small variety with pink flowers, and *S.* Sir D. Haig is a good crimson. *S.* Mrs Piper is a large deep salmony pink and *S.* Dartington Double has very full deep pink flowers.

For years I have grown *S. hypnoides gemmifera*, which used to be called *S. h. kingii*. It has very fine, light foliage and makes a hard tight cushion. The flowers are white, on slender stems, and it turns shades of crimson in autumn. I know nothing better for a completely solid cover and I do not know why it is no longer listed by nurserymen. Admittedly it is not as showy as the modern types, with their bright flowers, but for making a real carpet, which would be firm enough to walk on, it has no equal.

Almost as hearty as the mossy saxifrages, the rock phloxes make spreading mats and soon cover wide spaces. They become sheets of colour in the spring and are useful plants for growing on sunny banks and between autumn flowering shrubs. There are two kinds, *Phlox subulata* is the more exuberant and is known as the mossy phlox. Among the varieties in this group I like the soft lavender *P. s.* G. F. Wilson and *P. s.* Betty, which is a pink with large flowers. There are several other good pinks: Sprite, with a carmine eye, Samson and Model, both in a deep shade. The most brilliant of the lot, *P. s.* Temiscaming, must be carefully placed because it is almost violent in its intense deep red (or showy cerise, whichever you like). It makes a really gaudy splash of colour and needs the scene to itself.

The other type, *P. douglasii*, is neater in habit and its mats are about a foot square instead of 2 feet as in *P. subulata*. Again my favourite is a lavender: *P. d.* Boothman's Var. has small mauve flowers with violet centres. *P. d.* May Snow makes sheets of white flowers, *P. d. rosea* is a flat silvery-pink, and Eva, Gem and Violet Queen are all shades of lavender and purple. The *douglasii* types seldom need any attention but *P. subulata* needs trimming after flowering. Both types will root as they spread over the soil, *P. subulata* more than *P. douglasii*.

When I was given *Veronica peduncularis* Nyman's Var. I esteemed it because of loose showers of typical speedwell flowers. Its little blue flowers are lovely, but it is for its long trailing stems of evergreen leaves that I now admire it, for they make magnificent ground cover. A small plant in a north bed in my small front garden has spread its net to cover at least a square yard. This is in shade, and it does exactly the same in full sun in another part of the garden.

The woolly stems of *V. pectinata rosea* will cover the ground too and one plant should fill a space 15 inches square. In May and June the plants have sheets of pink flowers, whitish on the outside and deep rose within. *V. fruitcans* (*V. saxatilis*) is very neat and dwarf, with small dark leaves on prostrate stems, and in April and May bears spires of bright blue flowers, each with a red eye. It is actually a small shrub although it behaves like a herbaceous plant, and is long lived and slow-growing. Each plant covers a square foot, and it can be relied on to do its job well and not exceed its obligations.

The creeping *Hypericum reptans* is another low growing shrub that makes a good carpeting plant. It has many good qualities, like all the easy-to-please St John's Worts. Its evergreen foliage is fresh and bright and takes on a red-brown tinge in autumn, and from July to September it is covered with a succession of flat golden flowers.

I often wonder if it is the name that makes people so rude about *Cotula squalida**. It is actually a very attractive little creeping plant with delicate ferny foliage that hugs the ground and makes excellent cover for small bulbs. The minute flowers are a dull greeny-yellow, and that is where the offensive name comes in, for 'squalida' means dull yellow. The flowers are not striking, but they fit in very well with the creeping foliage and are certainly not unpleasant. The cotulas are definitely invasive; even *C. pyrethrifolia**, which was recommended to me as being better behaved than *C. squalida**, does not keep to the cracks in a paved path which I want it to fill, but wanders off to enjoy itself among my treasures in a well-nourished flower bed. These cotulas are tough, hard-wearing little plants and can be used to make lawns. There are other unidentified cotulas which are listed as cotula species. One of these has silky grey leaves, and in another the foliage is green and purple.

For quick and willing service the acaenas are hard to beat. We are often advised not to admit them to a respectable rock garden, but as ground cover no one would gainsay their attractiveness. The pale green carpets of *A. buchananii* have burr-like flowers the same colour as the leaves; in *A. glauca** the leaves and flowers are particularly delightful as a cover for blue-flowered bulbous plants. The other green-leaved acaena is *A. sanguisorbae**, so called because of its healing qualities. The purple flowers of this variety are rather small.

The bronze-leaved acaenas make rich pools of colour, and are even richer when covered with blood red or purple burrs. In *A. microphylla* the spiny crimson burrs are particularly vicious, attaching themselves to anything available, as anyone who may casually kneel on a patch while weeding has reason to remember. The foliage of *A. m. inermis** has pink and purple hints in the bronze of its leaves and the purple flowers are less harmful. (The meaning of 'inermis' is unarmed.) The third bronze acaena is *A. novae-zealandiae** and its purple flowers are distinguished by having barbed spines.

The silver-leaved antennarias are often used as cover for bulbs. The prettiest is *A. dioica rosea*, with little fluffy pale pink flowers in tight heads. This small tufted plant is seldom more than 2 inches high, although in *A. d. tomentosa** the creamy-white flowers are on 3-inch stalks, amid silver foliage, and *A. d. rubra* with rosy-red flowers is the same height. Each plant will make a carpet about a foot square.

Helichrysum bellidioides is another little creeping plant about 6 inches high. It makes quite a solid mat of small green leaves lined with silver and has clusters of white everlasting flowers on short stems. It will soon spread to make an 18-inch clump.

With foliage rather like a heather, frankenia is a mat-forming plant which makes a 12-inch plant. I like best *F. laevis*, which turns shades of crimson and orange in autumn and has stemless small pink flowers. In *F. thymifolia* the leaves are more like thyme than heather and the pink flowers are larger and more plentiful.

Other good creeping plants are *Mazus reptans*, which roots as it goes and from its close mat produces large flowers, not unlike those of the lobelia, in mauve, with orange speckled white throats. A plant will cover 18 inches square. *Herniaria glabra* becomes a shiny green carpet, not unlike thyme, which turns bronze in sun.

Hippocrepis comosa is a good plant for light limy soil in sun. It is one of our British native plants and makes a close mat of neat foliage, about 18 inches in diameter, and has pea-like flowers in bright gold. In *H. c.* E. R. Janes the flowers are lemon-yellow. Both have the horse-shoe-shaped seedpods which give the plant its name. *Hydrocotyle moschata* with its glossy leaves is a good carpeter for a shady position.

The saginas are good carpeting plants, making mats of short glossy foliage and small starry white flowers. They increase very consistently and will cover any given space in quite a short time. *S. glabra* is the green-leaved form; in *S. g. aurea* the foliage is golden, and both are strongly scented of violets.

For quick cover the tiny creeping *Lippia canascens* (*L. repens*) is a good plant to choose. It does not take long to cover a square yard of soil, particularly in a sheltered position. It has mauve-pink scabious flowers, and in *L. c. alba* the flowers are white.

Pratia treadwellii takes a little longer to increase and needs time to make a fairly thick carpet, rooting as it goes, but it is then good cover with its small round leaves. The stemless white flowers are like small lobelias and are marked with crimson and are followed by quite large purple berries. Very often flowers and berries are on the plants at the same time. I have grown this plant both in sun and shade and I have not found that it does better in one place or the other.

Some of the really tiny carpeting plants look quite fragile and yet are strangely tough and persistent. I am quite aware that I do not pay enough attention to *Epilobium macropus*, but it bears no malice and continues to spread quietly over a sunny pocket of the rock garden where brodiaeas are planted. When it gets to the stone at the edge of the pocket it still continues on its way, making a film of tiny leaves which turn crimson in the autumn.

Arenaria balearica has a little more substance and needs to be started in shade. After it has got a foothold it may come out into the sun and then there is no stopping it. It has the tiniest leaves of almost any plant I know and yet it will cover wide areas of soil, stone or wall with its carpet of green, to be studded in early summer with myriads of small stars of white.

It took me many years to get *Raoulia australis* to grow for me, and yet I have seen it spreading over quite large areas of open well-drained rock garden where bulbs were planted. When at last it consented to grow for me it was at the edge of a gravel path, and now it is covering all the ground (and stone) round a large clump of the glaucous grass, *Helictotrichon sempervirens*. Nearby grows the pink, purple and bronze *Acaena microphylla inermis** and the two together are very pretty. *Raoulia lutescens* is even smaller and its film of grey-green has tiny golden flowers, which have to be scrutinised through a magnifying glass if one is to enjoy them. *R. tenuicaulis* is also grey-green and when it finds a place it likes will spread quite well. All the raoulias make carpets about a foot square, that is except for *R. lutescens* which seldom grows quite so big.

The tiny silver and green leaves of *Sibthorpia europaea variegate* glisten in a cool spot; *Linaria aequitriloba* is a little bigger and has tiny mauve flowers. For damp shady places where something small is needed the miniature form of creeping jenny, *Lysimachia japonica minuta* can be used. It makes a very close mat of neat green foliage and is studded with stemless open yellow flowers.

The trouble with some plants is that they do their job so well that they become a menace. Such a plant is *Helxine soleirolii*, sometimes known as Corsican Curse. There are certain places only where it could possibly be planted. If one happened to have a dark, dank courtyard which needed the softening influence of tender green, nothing could be more charming than helxine. It is very good bright green and its tiny green leaves are almost lacquered, and one needs a magnifying glass to find the tiny flowers. In damp shade it will work up walls, fill all the odd corners with fresh green, and work along cracks in paving so that each is outlined. Put it anywhere near a flower bed and it will hop in while one's back is turned and once there it stays, however often one skims it from the soil. Though a hard frost will give it such a beating that it looks quite dead, it usually survives and starts pushing in as hard as ever.

I grow both the golden and variegated forms, and they do not increase as much as one would like them to. I find it very difficult to keep them from being swamped by the green menace. How it gets in I cannot tell, unless the two rarer forms do not seed true. It is very difficult to get rid of the green without sacrificing some of the rare golden or variegated types, and if one scrap of green is overlooked it will start infiltrating all over again.

~ 6 ~
Rampers

The quickest and most effective ground cover plant I know is the alpine strawberry. It is a good worker too, and pays dividends in delicious fruit from May to November – if one has time and energy to pick it. It is not particularly beautiful, but makes a shaggy green carpet brightened by the glinting crimson of the berries. But it is a plant that knows no bounds and pokes its nose into places where it is not wanted, and once it is admitted to a garden it has to be treated very firmly if it is not to take over completely.

There is another strawberry that is nearly as bad, *Fragaria indica**, sometimes called *Duchesnea*. From an aesthetic angle it has more attractions, its leaves are a good dark green, the yellow flowers turn to luscious red berries, which belie their magnificence by being absolutely tasteless. Even the birds leave them alone, so the display goes on for many weeks. The long trails, which root wherever they touch down, are popular for hanging baskets and I wonder the flower arrangers have not taken it up more enthusiastically. It can become a nuisance if unchecked but it is easily removed.

If *Lamium galeobdolon variegatum* were not so lovely I think it might get some black looks, because it has no idea that there are places in the garden where it is not wanted. It too is a trailer and it trails in a big way, flinging itself down banks, under trees and anywhere else it sees a nice clear space. But it takes the rough with the smooth, and planted at the edge of a gravel path it will work its way along the bottom of walls and buildings, making a pleasant and graceful swirl of green in a place where weeds often grow. It takes away the hard lines of stone and softens corners. The soft grey-green leaves are always good, with their silver markings, and they become more brilliant in winter, almost dazzlingly bright just at the time when such splendour is most needed. I could do without the flowers which are typical yellow dead nettles, quite pretty, but I think they detract from the beauty of the leaves, and I am glad they have one quick blooming only instead of flowering on and off all through the year like the other lamiums.

This lamium may be invasive, but it is a surface rooter, so that it is a wonderful plant for covering the ground under trees where bulbs are planted, and it is easily removed, unlike another most determined invader, *Cerastium tomentosum*. The lamium is straightforward in its dealings and works in the open, but Snow on the Mountains, as the villagers call this insidious worker, comes creeping in below the surface, and with its tangle of determined little white roots is extremely difficult to eradicate if it goes too far. It is a pity that a plant which is so effective in the garden has to be kept to places where it can be controlled. Its close mat of small woolly foliage with white flowers above makes it one of the best silver cover plants in the garden, and if it can be used where it can increase as much as it wants there is nothing better. It can be used on walls, under trees where the soil is poor and dry, and on banks where there are no limitations as to how far it can run.

Some of the bugles can be rather overpowering, particularly the green *Ajuga reptans*. It has much to recommend it, fresh glossy rosettes which are evergreen and always attractive, and sturdy spikes of blue flowers. It works hard all the time sending out stems in all directions with fleshy rosettes at the end of each, and is probably more luxuriant in shade, although if it finds itself in the sun it does not sulk. There is an attractive form with white flowers, perhaps not quite so luxuriant as the type, but an industrious worker which soon makes a solid mat of bronzed green. The red-leaved bugle, *A. r. rubra*, is also luxuriant and so is *A. r. multi-color**, which has metallic variations and is sometimes called *A.* Tortoiseshell or *A.* Rainbow. The variegated from of bugle is a smaller, less rampant plant. It will make a good cover but it takes longer to do it. *A. pyramidalis* is a most attractive plant, with particularly good bright blue flower spikes, but it increases slowly and has to be increased by divisions as it does not send out runners.

A sedum which never knows where to stop has its uses when large rough areas need an attractive cover. *S. spurium* has strong fleshy stems which make a solid mat on the surface of the soil and are covered with fleshy leaves and flat heads of pink flowers. There is a form with white flowers and in *S. s.* Schorbusser Blut the flowers are blood red and the leaves turn crimson in autumn.

In a position where it has all the room it wants *Campanula poscharskyana* is an ally, covering much space with bright green foliage and has 18-inch trails of flower for most of the summer. It will grow in sun or shade and in any soil, in fact the only time I have any complaints about it is when I make the mistake of planting it where it can swamp less robust plants. The white form is not quite so robust as the type – like many other plants with white flowers – and makes a welcome change.

C. portenschlagiana is just as pushing but does not make quite such a shaggy cover, because it has smaller leaves and grows in a more compact way. But it has the same fine white roots, which look innocent but are none the less capable of the utmost penetration into friendly territory. It is very easily broken up into small pieces, and these planted in sand and peat will soon join up and make an impenetrable mat which will keep spreading at the edges. Sometimes known as

*C. muralis**, this campanula is often seen on walls or among stones, but it will make a wonderful ground cover in sun or shade in good soil or poor, and after its main flowering in late May and early June it goes on producing odd flowers all through the season. For a smaller space *C. garganica* is quite useful, it will fill its given corner with very tight growth and has light blue star-like flowers. While on the subject of campanulas, I think *C. glomerata* should be recommended for shady places under trees although its running roots put it in the category of rampers. Also it furnishes patches of a rich deep blue, which is not a very common colour in the garden. The compact rounded heads of the clustered bell flowers top 15-inch sturdy stems. There is a useful dwarf form, *C. g. acaulis**, which has a white counterpart, again a little less robust than the blue one.

I would call *C. latiloba* a ramper, it certainly is with me and seems to make a wide clump in a very short time. I am always finding stretches of its tufted green leaves in places where I certainly never planted it. It has the family root structure and is easy to divide and increase. It will send up its 18-inch flower spikes in the most inauspicious places, the arid soil under hollies or poplars, the dry soil under walls, and I am sure would have a shot at covering any piece of waste soil. In these cases I find no difference in the energy of the blue and white forms.

The various forms of *Vinca minor* grow well, but they are so neat that I would not call them rampers; however there are two periwinkles which are definitely invasive, *V. acutiloba* and *V. major*. The former has very long stems and can therefore start establishing itself within a radius of a yard or more from its base. Each time it comes to earth it makes a neat little plant with pink stems from which it throws up flower stems topped with angular slate-blue flowers in autumn and winter. It is evergreen, and though its leaves are smaller than those of *V. major*, when the stems criss and cross there is a cover thick enough to keep out weeds. It is much used under trees in the National Trust garden, Hidcote, in Gloucestershire.

There is nothing half-hearted or halting about *V. major*. The leaves are large and glossy and I have never seen them at any time in the year when they looked anything but sleek and unperturbed. This vinca is a quicker worker and each of its new 'touch-down' plants is composed of several strong shoots, so that there is soon a forest. It is a wonderful plant for fitting in spaces under trees, on banks, or if you have a hedge that is bare at the base, this periwinkle will thicken up and produce large, innocent blue flowers of a Wedgwood shade of blue. The variegated form, *V. m. variegate* (*elegantissima*), is not quite as rampant as its green counterpart, but it can do a very good job if left to itself. The cream splashed leaves look particularly pleasant between dark shrubs, grown with *Cotoneaster horizontalis* or cascading down banks under trees.

One of the most commonly used plants when dense luxuriant ground cover is needed is *Hypericum calycinum*. It is a most reliable plant but it is not one to plant unless one is absolutely certain that one will not change one's mind about it later on, for once it has a foothold it is not easily removed. It is an attractive plant with good foliage and bright yellow flowers. It is improved by a drastic trimming in the spring. Its height is a good 12 inches and its spread 'indefinite' – quoting from a reference book. It flowers from June to October, and if one does not mind a plant that will run like mad whenever it finds itself in a nice shady spot the Rose of Sharon is the plant to choose.

Pachysandra terminalis is regarded as a rampant ground cover by many people, although it does not ramp in my garden. This is the plant the Americans use to make carpets of green under their trees. In so many American gardens the natural trees are left and simply under-planted with pachysandra and English ivy, and certainly the effect is pleasing and furnished at all times of the year. On all sides I hear recommendations of *P. terminalis* as a super ground cover, so perhaps it does better for other people than for me. It makes a thick planting of rather fleshy green leaves 9 inches to 1 foot high, with whitish flowers in February and March. When it grows well there is nothing more reliable; it is as regular as a field of corn, it makes a level sward of greyish-green.

A rampant variegated grass, *Phalaris arundinacea picta*, is useful in certain places, and though to keep it as a carpet and not a thicket means it must be cut down from time to time, I think the work involved is not wasted. Large shears can be used and then the tight mat of fresh green and white is very pleasing under the shade of trees or between tall, bold plants in a border. Gardener's Garters is the old name for this grass, which is also known as Ribbon Grass. It makes a dense and woody mass of root and stem which discourages even perennial weeds. Among tall shrubs it can be left untrimmed so that the 3-foot striped leaves can make good contrast. They turn to deep ivory in the winter and remain attractive till the spring.

Perhaps rampant is rather too strong a term to use about our native woodruff, *Asperula odorata**, and 'spreading' might be better. For it does spread very satisfactorily in a shady, damp spot. The narrow green leaves are rather dark and grow in whorls up slender stems, studded with small white-starred flowers. The foliage smells deliciously of new-mown hay and when cut and dried retains its fragrance.

I do not call the running euphorbia, *E. cyparissias*, a ramper either, probably because I like it very much and could not imagine having too much of it. But I have friends who regard it as a nuisance, particularly if it gets a foothold in crazy paving. There it can be a nuisance, running hither and yon under the stones and popping up in every crevice. These adventurous qualities make it a most successful ground cover plant. I grow it under conifers, among ivies where its rather pale green ruffled stems and yellow-green flower heads contrast well with the silver-blue of the conifers. It is the 'ploughman's mignonette' of cottage gardens, a simple unassuming plant, irresistible to those of us who like green flowers.

Those dwarf and sturdy pygmy michaelmas daisies that increase too fast for ordinary borders make unusual and colourful ground cover and one likes them better when not faced with the yearly agony of having to dig up and discard the unoffending creatures by the square yard. How often we admire the wide borders of mauve or pink in autumn. They grow evenly and thickly, and if instead of straight borders they are planted to fill in the space between trees and shrubs (wide plantings that taper off into the background), no cover could be more effective or more colourful. New varieties appear every year, but some of the older ones are very reliable. Victor in light blue, and Little Baby Blue, are under 9 inches, Lady in blue about 10 inches, and Lilac Time the same height. The pale pink Rosebud and Peter Harrison in deeper pink are good, while Snow Cushion* provides a background of white.

Veronica filiformis is the gardener's curse, and though it is artless and pretty it must be avoided. A well-known nursery offers it with the admission that it is 'frankly invasive, but lovely' – I was given it as a treasure and at first I enjoyed its film of green, covered with typical speedwell flowers. Then it began filming over other beds, it got into the lawn, and there were little blue flowers all among the grass; from there it found other beds to decorate. In a completely wild and untamed part of the garden its attractiveness could be tolerated; in cultivated gardens, never.

~ 7 ~
Coloured Foliage

Not only do different shapes and texture help a garden, but leaves of different colours all help the picture and prevent monotony.

Useful contrasts can be achieved by choosing under-planting to contrast with the shrubs or plants with which they are used. Red and bronze look well with silver shrubs, just as a silver carpet is good under red-leaved shrubs such as purple rhus, *R. cotinus foliis purpureis*, which is now known as *Cotinus coggygria purpureus**, or the purple *Berberis thunbergii atropurpurea**.

Glaucous plants look well against very dark green, golden foliage can be used where a suggestion of sunshine is needed, variegated subjects show up best in dark places, and a gentle picture is made by mixing greys, soft greens and bluish downy foliage such as is found in *Salvia sclarea turkestanica*. Dorynicum is a dwarf spreading shrub which can be planted to cover the ground in front of the salvias, with the soft light green of *Phlomis fruticosa* in the background.

PURPLE, BRONZE AND RED

The best red-leaved carpeter is undoubtedly the red bugle, *Ajuga rubra*. It really is red and is very colourful, particularly in the winter. I like to use it under the silver *Senecio laxifolius* or as a background to the frothy silver of *Artemisia* Lambrook Silver* or *Centaurea gymnocarpa**. The purple-leaved viola, *V. labradorica*, is an excellent plant for ground cover. It makes good-sized clumps and sows itself about, but does not take much from the soil so is even safe to use under roses. The soft blue flowers are not scented, alas, but they are very pretty and come and go for a long time.

The purple-leaved clover, *Trifolium repens pentaphyllum*, is not very tough and takes a little time to thicken up, but in a conspicuous place that is not too large it makes a pleasing cover. Many of the leaves have four leaflets, they are edged with green, and the typical clover flowers are oatmeal coloured.

If the flower spikes are kept cut the bronze-leaved plantain makes good cover because the roots are strong and the beetroot-coloured leaves quite big. The plants should be put fairly close together and soon colonise if all the spikes are not removed very quickly. This is something I always mean to do but often fail to achieve early enough and the result is innumerable seedlings in different parts of the garden.

Mounds of purple sage are attractive between all the plants that come and go. In time this sage, *Salvia officinalis purpurascens*, makes rather a big bush and then it is time to take it out and start again. It comes very easily from cuttings.

Not all purple, but with many blotches of maroon on its dark green leaves, *Hieracium maculatum* is rather an unusual plant and makes a rich background. I cut off the flowers, which are typical golden hawkweed and quite unworthy of the plant. Also if they are left on one gets rather too many seedlings.

The dwarf form of *Berberis thunbergii atropurpurea** named *nana* does not spread very much, the 2-foot shrubs making bushes about 3 feet across, but this dome of rich foliage acts as ground cover as well as adding rich colour to the border.

Primroses with purple leaves are, I always think, wasted if planted in ordinary beds without contrasting foliage to show up the richness of the leaves. Sometimes the crinkled leaves of *Primula* Garryarde Guinevere are hardly discernible against a dark soil, but if I gardened on the Berkshire downs I should grow this primrose very often to cover tracts of the depressing putty-coloured soil. It is the best of the garryardes, I think, for ground cover, because it grows quickly and produces many lilac-pink flowers. *P.* Buckland Primrose, with deep ivory flowers, *P.* The Pilgrim and *P.* The Grail also have purplish leaves. The flat, crinkled leaves of *P.* Wisley Red are particularly rich in colour. It is a tiny plant, which grows absolutely flat on the ground and soon makes a solid carpet of small leaves, with small purplish red flowers on short stalks. There is another small primrose very similar which was grown by a Mr F. Ashby and is called *P.* F. Ashby. It has flowers a little more crimson than *P.* Wisley Red.

GOLDEN

Golden marjoram is one of the best of the golden ground cover plants. *Origanum vulgare aureum* makes a close heavy mat of small golden leaves which are evergreen, and the best from for good ground cover is the curled variety. There is another gold marjoram, but it has typical marjoram pointed leaves and never seems to grow quite so robustly as the other.

One of the brightest little golden carpeting plants is the golden form of Creeping Jenny, *Lysimachia nummularia aurea*. It is supposed to need a damp position, and though it would probably grow much faster in damp soil it seems to do very well in any garden soil. I have seen it making carpets of sunshine under a garden bridge, and on ledges in dark corners it will bring a welcome gleam of gold.

The golden lamium, *L. maculatum aureum*, is not so reliable or quick growing as the other dead nettles. It is not deciduous but it often looks rather miserable in winter. Unlike most golden-leaved plants it seems to do better in shade than in sun. I have tried it in many places in the garden and have been on the edge of losing it several times. It furnishes beautiful golden foliage but it is not a plant for wide areas or tough places. I find it does best in shady spots on banks or at the bottom of walls. It tends to get bare in places and then I think it needs to be top-dressed with sand and peat.

The golden mint, *Mentha* × *gentiles aurea*, is not evergreen but it makes a thicket of foliage in the summer months. Sometimes called the ginger mint, it is very aromatic but is an even worse runner than ordinary mint. One puts up with it because it is such an attractive plant, bringing sunshine into dark corners and scenting the air around.

Another herb with good golden variegations is balm or Lemon Balm as the cottagers call it, and the full name of the golden variegated variety is *Melissa officinalis aurea*. Ordinary balm can be a nuisance with its persistent seeding, but the golden from does not seed, has larger leaves and makes a thick, close mat. It is at its golden best in full sun and before the flower stalks appear. If I had time I would not let it flower but would cut off every flowering stem, because it is for its golden carpet I grow it, and though there are glints of gold among the flowers they are a poor imitation of the early growth.

Mr Bowles' golden grass, *Milium efusum aureum*, looks rather a delicate little thing, but it is really quite tough and small plants soon thicken into solid clumps. It seeds itself too – tiny golden scraps that look as if the wind would blow them away but which soon became grown-up plants – so that it soon makes a carpet of gold. It is particularly effective in spring when leaves, stems and flowers are bright gold, and it does best in shade, so is an ideal plant for dark corners. It can grow to 2 feet, but with me it is seldom more than a foot or 18 inches, which means that it is a dwarf enough to keep tidy.

*Alopecurus pratensis foliis variegatis**, Foxtail, has gold-striped leaves about a foot high and it makes a rough, rather untidy looking plant until the flower spikes grow. But in the distance its bronze effect is good.

The golden snowberry, *Symphoricarpos orbiculatus variegates*, is a bigger plant altogether, but it can make quite useful ground cover among dark shrubs or even perennials in the herbaceous border. It usually grows to about 3 feet and unlike the ordinary snowberry does not sucker. But it does throw out long stems which root wherever they touch the ground. If I am growing this little bush as a specimen plant above low-growing plants I cut off the suckering stems and replant the rooted pieces elsewhere. But if the idea is ground cover the shrub can be allowed to layer itself as much as it wants and will soon be spreading in all directions. It is quite an attractive shrub with small pointed leaves margined irregularly with gold.

GLAUCOUS

The blue leaves of glaucous plants make a very pleasant variation among the greens, and one of the best for covering large areas is *Othonnopsis cheirifolia*. I have never seen any connection between this plant and wallflowers, so I cannot understand its second name. Its leaves are flat and paddle-shaped and come in layers and the flowers are yellow daisies, thick set and rather small, but they go with the plant and are early. In a normal winter this plant is quite unaffected, so it is a good choice for the front of beds or other places in the garden which are in view most of the time. It is seldom more than 9 inches high but can spread to cover any area. The long arms stretch out in all directions and root as they touch the ground, and from this new plant more shoots emerge to increase the plant still further. After some years the middle of the plant may become a little bare and shabby, and then one performs a surgical operation (to take its stomach out, as an old friend of mine used to say) and fills the empty space with some of the new plants from the outside. If it is desired to get a lot of new plants quickly for clothing other places the rooting habits of the plant can be encouraged by putting sand on the soil under the stems and some flat stones on top of the stems. It is also quite easy to increase one's stock by cuttings. I always grow it in full sun, but I have seen it in walls and on banks in light shade.

Rue (*Ruta graveolens*), particularly the form Jackman's Blue, has very blue ferny leaves and is a most decorative contrast to foliage of other colours. It contrasts well with purple sage, and blends with the golden sage or soft green of *Alchemilla mollis*. The small bushes are usually about 18 inches high and tend to spread as they grow, making informal mounds of finely cut, aromatic blue leaves.

The fine spiky leaves of dianthus cover quite considerable tracts of ground and make a patch of good glaucous foliage. Such strains as Highland Hybrids make excellent ground cover plants, as they soon make plants at least a foot across, and produce their single flowers on 10-inch stems through early summer. The flowers have maroon centres and range from white to deep pink. Another variety that makes a heavy mat is the green-centred single white, Musgrave's White*, sometimes called Green Eyes. Sometimes large pinks such as Thomas make wide plants of strong, very glaucous foliage. I have a single red dianthus which came from Brympton d'Evercy and is now known as Brympton Red. The flowers are carried on foot high stems and the foliage is very close and rather fine, which makes it an excellent plant for making glaucous ground cover. Even the old clove pink can be used. It has wider, stronger leaves and they are particularly good in colour. Pinks are good plants for use among shrub roses and can be used at the edge of rose beds set in paving to soften the edges.

All pinks become straggling after a time. They need cutting back each year when they get untidy, but the time comes when they have to be replaced with small new plants. Cuttings taken in July root quickly in a cold frame.

The sedums too make patches of beautiful blue-grey colour. Although *Sedum spectabile* reaches a foot or more when in flower it is completely dwarf for many months and those tight-packed neat rosettes make wonderful cover. It is a most compact and well-behaved plant, increasing steadily, and in the end will fill all the space available. It is very easily increased because each small piece will grow, and is a trouble-free plant all through its life.

The palest flowered sedum is *S. s. roseum*, which is taller than *S. spectabile* and has paler flowers. Hybrids of *S. spectabile* such as Autumn Joy, Meteor, Carmen and Brilliant all make thick, neat covers, and so does *S. telephium* Munstead Red, but *S. maximum atropurpureum* is rather looser in growth.

The large wrinkled leaves of *Hosta sieboldiana* (*glauca*) are a wonderful shade of blue-green, and are beautiful under trees or among shrubs during the summer months. In early April the pointed shoots make their appearance, soon to unfurl to large heart-shaped leaves.

There are several glaucous grasses, the 18-inch *Helictotrichon sempervirens* makes an imposing clump of graceful glaucous narrow leaves. The dwarf *Festuca ovina*, a form of Sheep's Fescue, is also good for ground cover. It grows in dense tufts of glaucous narrow leaves.

The tall *Elymus glaucus** increases so fast that it can be considered as ground cover where the soil is poor and the landscape wide. It is an outstanding plant, with its 4-foot stems and rather stiff flower spikes, but it needs room.

The loose swirls of ferny foliage that adorn the long and adventuring stems of *Acaena adscendens** are very distinct in colour, almost as blue as verdigris, but lovely in contrast to the rich mahogany of *Sedum maximum atropurpureum* or *Lobelia fulgens*. The first time I saw it it had escaped from the corner of a terrace bed and was covering a wide area of gravel path. It is a generous plant and is wasted if it has not a good expanse to cover.

GREY

Grey leaves can be very restful. We use many silver plants in the garden and they give sparkle and accent we could not do without, but we need the quiet harmony of soft greys as well. A carpet of the woolly thyme, *Thymus serpyllum lanuginosus* (sometimes called *T. lanuginosus*), is good in hot dry places and the soft woolly leaves are excellent in contrast to glossy foliage or the shiny metallic leaves of *Ajuga reptans multicolor**. It has pink flowers but does not often produce them.

Veronica pectinata rosea, on the other hand, flowers extremely well, and there are many little bright pink speedwell flowers among the sprawling stems covered with small grey woolly leaves. It does not make such a dense cover as the thyme.

Pterocephalus parnasii, which we used to know as *Scabiosa pterocephaus*, has soft grey-green leaves and it packs its foliage together in a tight cushion, studded with soft lavender scabious flowers in July and August.

To use *Ballota pseudodictamnus* as ground cover it should be kept low and spreading, and then it will cover a good square yard or more. It is usually quite attractive in the winter, unless the weather is exceptionally severe, and its round woolly leaves in soft grey-green look cosy. Flower arrangers like the long flower stems with little woolly calyces tight against the woody stem. In the centre of each cup is a small lavender-pink flower. For myself I prefer the plants without the flowering stems, which always seem to make them untidy, and am always glad when I can cut them off. These stems always look rather bedraggled after rain, whereas the bushes themselves are always neat. It is easy to get up stocks by taking cuttings which root easily.

Grey is the colour of *Dorycnium hirsutum**. Seldom taller than a foot, it grows into a wide spreading bush which covers about a square yard or more. It needs a hot dry place and is useful on a bank or crouching on top of a wall. No weeds could survive under voluminous skirts, which seem to get thicker as the season advances. I described this plant as grey, and grey can sometimes be drab, which this plant most definitely is not. Its soft hairy leaves are an interesting shade of blue-grey and harmonise well with the pink and white pea flowers which open all through the summer.

The ferny foliage of *Anthemis cupaniana** is definitely grey. This plant, with its long straggling arms, covers a great deal of ground by the end of the season. The stems lie about on the ground, rooting here and there, and the result is a thick covering of fine grey foliage with a succession of large white daisies. It grows anywhere in sun or shade and can be used to cover the ground between shrubs or on top of a wall. It is another plant that is useful where sunny banks have to be covered.

Ground cover need not always be dwarf; a plant that makes a thicket and has impenetrable roots is useful under trees and between shrubs. *Artemisia pontica* has very delicate finely cut foliage, which is pewter grey for most of the year but is lighter in colour when the flowers open. It never grows more than about 1 foot to 18 inches and makes a series of spires like a closely packed cypress grove. The plant grows very closely and has such congested roots that it completely discourages all weeds. It is sometimes used to cover completely the ground under fruit trees. I noticed on one large garden the round beds in which apple trees were planted were covered completely with this artemisia.

The leaves of *Hebe pagei** are perhaps more glaucous than grey, but they are not the blue colour of such plants as rue and othonnopsis. But no small plant could make such reliable ground cover as this prostrate little shrub. It is completely indifferent to weather and its neat, mat-surfaced leaves grow on prostrate stems so that it makes excellent ground cover. One shrub soon covers a square yard of soil and more, and produces myriads of tiny spikes of white flowers. If top-dressed with peat many of the lower stems will root and can be detached to make new plants.

SILVER

There are many silver plants that make excellent ground cover; some are not evergreen, others do not always stand up to very bad weather. One of the most reliable is an old cottage plant, *Stachys lanata*, the favourite Lamb's Lugs of country gardens, with its large furry leaves and handsome flower spikes, also silver and covered with down. For ground cover it is usually best to cut off the flower stems and enjoy the close mat of velvety silver. This plant increases well by rooting its prostrate stems as they stretch further and further over the soil. It makes a very good border between flower bed and path, and is used to cover open spaces at the front of a border. In the white and silver garden of the National Trust garden Tintinhull, in Somerset, a wide planting of *S. lanata* links the paving round the pond with the four formal beds, planted with tall lilies, *Galtonica candicans, Artemisia* Silver Queen and the froth of *Cineraria maritima*.

There are several forms of *S. lanata* and I was recently given one that I am told never produces flowers. This is a good quality when it is ground cover we want, but I know gardeners who complain that they never get the tall branching flower stems which are so useful for drying.

Good winter ground cover is given by several of the silver plants that make evergreen rosettes. In the summer, of course, the plants will be in flower and though they still cover the ground one has to reckon with growth that is often tall. *Anaphalis triplinervis* makes tight clumps of neat silver foliage which is pleasant to see in the winter and spring. In early summer it starts to send out foot high flower spikes, which produce their small, ivory daisies in late summer. The little flowers with their golden centres dry well, but they also dry well on the plant. This is a good plant for filling in between taller plants; it will fill all the space it is offered and need not be cut down till very late in the year because the flowers remain attractive, in fact I always find it difficult to cut them off at all.

Lychnis coronaria has longer, bigger leaves, and its silver clumps are 5 or 6 inches high before it thinks of flowering. But a close planting of these handsome tufted plants is a good way of covering ground that is bare in winter. I grow the white-flowered Rose Campion as well as the normal magenta-flowered type or the more crimson *L. coronaria* Abbotswood Rose. As well as the pure white form there is a charming white variety with pink centres.

Another lychnis that can be used in small areas is *L.* Cottage Maid, a much smaller plant, with candy pink flowers on 12-inch stalks. It has much smaller leaves and makes spreading mats, so is ideal as a ground cover plant. I use it under dwarf roses because it takes little from the soil and its flowering period is comparatively short and it does not go on all the summer as *Lychnis coronaria* does. *L.* Cottage Maid is the same as *L. flos-jovis*, but one has to be wary when buying it. When I first started gardening I bought *L. flos-jovis* and was sent Bouncing Bet (*Saponaria officinalis*)! I am still waging war on this lady, knowing I cannot possibly win, whereas the demure little Cottage Maid has no predatory ways and receives blessings instead of cursings.

The large felted leaves of *Verbascum bombyciferum* (*V.* Broussa) makes most handsome ground cover in the winter. These rosettes lie flat on the ground and are about 2 feet across, startlingly white, and untouched by caterpillars, which ruin their beauty in the summer. *V. haenseleri* is also silver but its leaves are smaller and more silky than downy. The rosettes are smaller and not so dazzlingly white in the winter, but caterpillars do not appear to like them, so I now grow this mullein instead of the more spectacular *V. bombyciferum*.

Even more showy than the verbascums, large plants of the cotton thistle, *Onopordon acanthium*, can make a startling show in winter. The enormous leaves with their fluted, spiny edges lie flat on the ground; they are very white and will easily cover about 2 feet square. These thistles sow themselves in awkward places and must be replanted as soon as possible as they become more unpleasant to handle as they get bigger. They cannot be planted too close together because the full-grown plants with their 12-foot stems and 6-foot arm span take up a good deal of room, and no one wants to have too many of them anyhow, unless one is going in for a ghost garden!

Most of the creeping silver plants are best for full sun, the little silver *Artemisia pedemontana**, for instance, which literally walks over the ground. Its fine narrow leaves are silky and though it has such a delicate air when it finds itself in the light, sandy soil it prefers, with the sun overhead, it is soon a thick silver carpet. At Knightshayes Court, near Tiberton, it is used as ground cover in a formal garden that used to be planted with irises and now has bergenias and silver plants. *A. schmidtii** is another plant of the same type which does very well for some people but in my garden often disappears in the winter, although I can usually keep *A. pedemontana**. From this it will be seen that these artemisias are not hard-wearing ground cover plants that will ramp anywhere, but will provide elegant cover in special places if one can provide the right conditions.

*Chrysanthemum haradjanii** I would put in the same category. This is another of the silver plants that is used at Knightshayes to cover the beds in the silver garden, and there it grows luxuriantly, making wide mats of almost white downy leaves, fringed like a fern. It is easily increased because the stems root as they touch the ground and have merely to be severed to make new plants.

There are more rampant, easily pleased silver ground cover plants. *Potentilla argentea* has rather small silver leaves and golden flowers, and it spreads quite quickly in a soil that is not too heavy. I would call *P. argyrophylla* a good ground cover plant for full sun, for its typical strawberry leaves are a good silver and the crowns grow very close to the ground. When the flowering stems are produced they also grow horizontally (unless it suits the scheme better to raise them and with supports train them to grow upright). A good plant of this potentilla will cover a square foot before it flowers and at least a square yard when in flower.

Veronica incana is another low growing silver plant that covers the ground quite freely. It has long narrow leaves and typical flower spikes of blue. It is a good subject to plant near the front of the border, where it can work backwards and sideways and even pour over the edge if the bed is a raised one.

Artemisia stelleriana makes a wonderful glistening white background in the summer but it is no good for winter effect, because by then its beautifully cut leaves, which are shaped like those of the chrysanthemum and make a lovely pattern on the soil, are bedraggled and tarnished. But all through the summer months the long trails can wind along sunny slopes and add greatly to the attraction of the planting.

The dwarf silver achilleas make good carpets in time, though not as speedily as some plants. *A. clavenae** produces its white flowers on 6 inch stems from June to October, *A. ageratifolia* has the same white and silver colour scheme, but in *A. prichardii* the foliage that goes with the white flowers is grey rather than silver. In *A. wilczeckiana** the finely serrated foliage is silver and it makes a good mat with white flowers on 12-inch stems.

I would not have thought of *Antennaria dioica* as a ground cover plant had I not sent it covering a square yard or more in a sunny rock garden. The foliage is very closely knit and as silver as any plant in the garden. The patch I saw had white flowers, and its correct name is *A. d. tomentosa**. It is not grown so often as *A. d. rosea* which has silvery-pink flowers. In both cases the flowers are fluffy and carried on 3-inch stems.

TRICOLOR

One of the most outstanding foliage plants is the tricolor form of *Hypericum* ×
moserianum and I have often recommended it for growing in conspicuous places
when something low and wide-growing is needed to cover as much of the bed as
possible. After two very cold winters I am a little shaken in my faith, for though
the hypericum did not actually die it was badly affected, and if we are going on
having very severe winters we shall have to revise our ideas of what to plant for
permanent ground cover. I should always want this hypericum in the garden,
because it has leaves of fantastic beauty, a mixture of cream, emerald and
crimson, and with its dwarf habit and wide spreading branches it covers about a
square yard and adds great beauty to the garden.

The leaves of the tricolor sage, *Salvia officinalis tricolor*, are the same
bluish-purple of the purple sage, but they are splashed with cream and
magenta-pink, and occasionally a dash of green for good measure. It grows
in the same way as the other sages, making pleasant spreading mounds which
can be kept low by judicious pruning and trimming. After several years the
bushes tend to get too big and sprawling, the stems become as thick as small
tree trunks, and then it is time to dig up the old bushes and fill the space with
several young plants, which will soon grow together and cover the same
amount of space. All the sages root very quickly from cuttings, and in the
case of the tricolor form it is important to choose cuttings with as distinct
variegation as possible.

Ajuga reptans Tortoiseshell is not really a tricolor, because the colouring is
more of a blend than a variegation. And it has more than three colours in its
leaves, which gives it its alternative name of *multi-color**. The background colour
is usually purplish, and there are glints of copper combined with cream, crimson
and gold, all with a curious metallic sheen. The colouring is most distinct when
the plant is grown in full sun.

VARIEGATED

Of all the carpeting variegated plants I think *Euonymus radicans* Silver Queen* is
the most distinct and reliable, although not the quickest to cover the ground. It
is evergreen and tough, the variegation is very clean and distinct, and, as its name
implies, it roots as it runs. I have a wide planting under a purple-leaved filbert,
and the contrast is very satisfactory.

Lamium galeobdolon variegatum has magnificent variegated foliage but because
of its exuberance it has to be classed as a ramper, Chapter Six. *L. maculatum* is less
persistent and confines itself to solid clumps. Its foliage is good all through the

year and it blooms in winter as well as summer, the form with mauve flowers blooms more freely than the forms with pink or white flowers.

Variegated ivies are dealt with in Chapter Fifteen, and variegated *Vinca major* in Chapter Six, as it is inclined to ramp, but variegated forms of *V. minor* are always restrained, although they make excellent ground cover. *V. m. argenteo-variegata* is the most common, with much silver in its pale green leaves and usually with blue flowers, although I believe there is a white-flowered form. *V. m. aureo-variegata* has rich golden variegations in yellow-green leaves, and the flowers can be white or blue, the white-flowered form being the most common. Though I have never seen it I believe there is another variegated form, *V. m. variegate*, with leaves having both gold and silver variegations.

Sometimes a stem or even the whole plant of the variegated form of *Sedum spectabile* will come plain and constant watch has to be kept to make sure it does not go back to green. It is always attractive, but I like it best in the early stages when the shoots of cream and grey-green make a tightly packed carpet. Like all the sedums it will pack solidly into any given space and allow no scope for weeds.

Another plant that is most attractive before it starts to grow up is the variegated form of apple mint, *Mentha rotundifolia variegate*. It is not, unfortunately, evergreen, but weeds do not grow where it is planted because of the dense tangle of thick roots just under the ground. In early spring when the lime-green and white leaves make their appearance it makes a delightful background for plants with dark green foliage. I am often tempted to cut off the flower stalks when they appear and this might have to be done if this mint is used as ground cover where only a carpet is wanted. But the tall stems with their pale variegated leaves are beautiful between plants with purple or very dark foliage, and are good for filling in spaces against a dense background. Some of the leaves are quite white, and the small, typically mint flowers are white too.

When I have spaces in prominent positions which I want to cover with good evergreen foliage I often use *Eryngium variifolium*, because for much of the year it is a solid mat of overlapping dark leaves, lightly variegated with white. These grow very close to the ground and increase quite well. In late summer tall flower spikes with stiff spider flowers in blue and silver rise to about 3 feet, and after they have been cut there still remains the solid mat of glossy evergreen leaves with their white markings.

The marbled leaves of *Arum pictum* (*corsicum**) are beautiful for many months of the year, but are not permanent cover. They come up in autumn and disappear again in late spring. There is nothing more lovely for a cool, leafy place in the garden and if the plants are undisturbed they soon increase to a colony, and produce stray seedlings in other parts of the garden. This is one of the plants that has definite likes about the place in which it wants to make its life. It grows well with me but never sows itself about, whereas in the garden of a friend in Sevenoaks it comes up everywhere. But never too often, for the handsome leaves furnish any spot, it never overlies other things and there is an unlimited demand for its leaves from flower arrangers.

There is another arum with veined and slightly mottled leaves, *A. italicum marmoratum**, which comes from S.E. Europe and the Canary Isles, and inevitably there is confusion between the two. I hope I am right in labelling my plants with larger, less distinctly marbled leaves. *A. italicum marmoratum*. It has to be well labelled because my plant could easily be a particularly good form of our native Lords and Ladies and I could easily remove it as a wild plant in the wrong place.

When I was given small plants of variegated cess, *Cardamine aurea**, I felt they would probably be more an annual proposition than a permanent feature, but not at all. Those delicate papery plants have come through tough winters and weathered ice and snow, like plants with leaves of leather. They are seeding themselves mildly in other parts of the garden and make very effective and unusual cover, with gold-splashed leaves in rounded hummocks. I think the effect would be better if I did not allow the plants to produce flower spikes, but then I would not get any seedlings!

Exciting effects in winter are achieved by the variegated figwort, *Scrophularia aquatica variegata*. At that time of the year the plant is making large and handsome rosettes on the surface of the ground, and there is little more outstanding than the distinct variegations of sparkling cream on pale green. Of course in the summer the tall flower spikes arise and merge with other plants, but by then the garden is a smother of flowers and leaves and no bare soil could be seen anyhow. Scrophularia is a foliage plant pure and simple; it has typical beady flowers the colour of a rodent's eye.

The variegated blackberry makes summer ground cover. It is often lost when grown as a conventional climber, and to appreciate its great beauty should, I think, be grown on the ground. I use it as ground cover on a bank at eye level at the top of the ditch, and it is at its magnificent best when the berries are red. Before they colour and when fully ripe they do not show up nearly so well. I grow it with a pink flowered pampas grass behind and a Ballawley Hybrid* bergenia on one side. When the blackberries are over the great crimson leaves of the bergenia give wonderful contrast. I peg the stems of the bramble to the ground with the hope that they will root as well as the tips of the stems, every one of which, of course, is pushed into the soil in the hope of a new plant.

Some of the dwarf variegated grasses make good ground cover. *Arrhenatherum elatius bulbosum variegatum** increases quite well but not at the rate of Ribbon

Grass, as Gardeners' Garters is sometimes called. It is delicately striped and always well behaved. It grows to about a foot and has bulbous roots which increase consistently. *Dactylis glomerata variegata*, Cocksfoot, is another foot-high grass striped with silver, and *Holcus lanatus variegatus* is dwarf and variegated. It grows in tufts and increases quite well.

~ 8 ~

Rhododendrons and Conifers

Because of my lime-laden soil I cannot grow rhododendrons unless I make special gardens for them. This limits me to small varieties and I have had a few flourishing specimens for many years, some in my small peat garden and others in a small patch of imported greensand under a north wall. That does not give me the right to speak about rhododenrons and I shall not mention many, but those that I do include are recommended by an expert. One of those I grow is *R. forrestii repens*, which would seem to be one of the first one would suggest for ground cover, but I am warned that it does not flower very freely and it should be recommended with this defect sufficiently stressed.

There are, I understand, many varieties of *R. forrestii repens* and I am told that some flower better than others, and the only safe way is to go by the seed packet number of the original plant and work on cuttings or layers from that.

I bought my first plant of this rhododendron when I made my peat garden nearly fifteen years ago. It came from a famous nursery which specialises in ericaceous plants, it has large leaves about 2 inches long and is absolutely prostrate. Even in peat I do not think it really likes my garden, although it produces a few blood-red flowers from time to time (more after a very cold winter). It has not increased much and I feel would be much more of a success in lime-free soil where it would cover large areas and doubtless flower more freely. The flowers always seem very large in proportion to the plant; they are bell-shaped and are borne singly or in pairs at the tips of its short branchlets.

Another form of this rhododendron, which is grown at Penheale Manor in Cornwall, has slightly smaller, more oval leaves and is a superlative ground cover plant. It completely covers a long bed under a wall, sloping against the wall and trying to get into the path, and it flowers magnificently. It is topdressed each year with peat and grows thicker every year. In another Cornish garden there are forms of *R. forestii repens*, some with leaves almost as narrow as rosemary and with everything in proportion. This rhododendron has the reputation for being a not very fast worker and it needs moist soil and partial shade if it is to do well.

Hybrids of *R. forestii repens* are usually better at flowering than the species itself. *R.* Elizabeth (*repens* × *griersonianum*) is low and spreading and has 3-

inch trumpet-shaped flowers in rich dark red, produced in clusters of five or six and opening in April. R. Little Ben (*neriiflorum* × *repens*) is a spreading shrub about 2 feet high which has brilliant scarlet flowers in April. R. Ethel (F. C. Puddle *x repens*) is also low and spreading with large crimson scarlet flowers in April.

Some of the R. *williamsianum* hybrids are good for ground cover and flower well. R. Treasure (*repens* × *williamsianum*) is a beautiful bush, wide for its height, with bell-shaped flowers in deep pink. In the well named R. Temple Belle (*orbiculare* × *williamsianum*) the flowers are pink and are described by nurserymen as Persian rose shade. R. *williamsianum* itself is fairly dwarf and rather the shape of a gigantic tea cosy, obliterating all weeds. With its small heart-shaped leaves and shell-pink flowers it is a wonderful sight when in full bloom. R. Humming Bird (*haematodes* × *williamsianum*) has crimson-pink flowers and though spreading the bushes may reach 4 feet in time.

Some gardeners do well with R. Blue Tit (*impeditum* × *augustinii*), others find that it does not flower too well and the colour of the flowers is not as good as R. Sapphire (*impeditum* type) or R. Intrifast (*intricatum* × *fastigiatum*), a good dwarf flue. They all make low, dense bushes good for ground cover.

Various forms of R. *lapponicum* such as *complexum* with purplish flowers, *fastigiatum* with lavender flowers and blue-green leaves, *impeditum* and *intricatum* grey-leaved and lavender flowered, are all good for ground cover.

R. *saluenense* provides some useful low varieties. R. *keleticum* makes mats of very small leaves from which the flat, purple-crimson flowers arise singly or in pairs. R. *calostrotum* is about a foot high only and has grey leaves and large, flat, bright magenta-crimson flowers. A low thick carpet can be made with R. *radicans*, which has small bright green leaves and flattish purple flowers in May.

The alpenrose of Switzerland, R. *ferrugineum*, is one of the best rhododendrons for covering the ground and it does not insist on lime-free soil, although I always give it plenty of peat when I plant it. It is rather an irregular shaped bush, and its informal growth makes it pleasant in a large rock garden or in a big paved terrace. The foliage is bright green and is even lighter and brighter in spring when the new growth starts. The flowers, which open in June, are rosy crimson and not very big. The white form is delightful too but not so often seen.

Great care should be taken when planting rhododendrons (just as with ericas and daboecias) to see that the ground is absolutely free of perennial weeds, for once the shrubs are settled in it is very difficult to get rid of such weeds.

CONIFERS

Some of the low-growing conifers make wonderful ground cover, which is hard-wearing and colourful, and can be relied on to give no trouble when once established.

A prostrate conifer is a good choice for covering the soil at corners of borders where paving runs beside the bed and something flat and yet wide is needed to give a feeling of spaciousness and stability. It creates a feeling of permanence too, for conifers in the garden mean that it is old and established and not just a creation of annuals and bedding plants only. The annual display can be used as well and will look all the better for the conifer mats.

For years I have enjoyed the beautiful variegated *Juniperus chinensis expansa variegate*. It is a horizontal conifer, in bright green, with white tips to the branches. It started as a 6-inch plant which I used at the bottom of a sundial to make a flat green carpet. Now it covers quite a wide space and has worked its way up the column of the sundial, as well as spreading out over the bed. The foliage of conifers goes well with stone, which needs dense strong leaves sometimes to prevent it looking too hard. There is nothing flimsy about conifers and being evergreen the effect is pleasing all through the year.

While my pet ground cover juniper is smooth enough for the most tailored garden I would not use the mat-forming juniper, *J. conferta* (*litoralis*), in a small, neatly planted garden but would prefer it in a woodland setting or under trees. It has rather a tough, uneven appearance and looks better in fairly large plantings. It comes from the sandy sea-shores of Japan, which may be why it has the look of being ruffled by the wind. *J. horizontalis douglasii* has rather the same look in winter when its whip-like branches turn purple. *J. h. plumose* is dense and flat-topped, light green in colour and usually about 18 inches high.

The low-growing conifer I would use for wide, important spaces is *J. communis saxatilis* (*J. c. hornibrookii*), growing from 6 inches to 3 feet high. It has flat branches of grey-green which gradually pile up one on top of each other as the bush ages. Another juniper that is excellent for ground cover is *J. c. nana prostrata*.

For large areas where something a little higher as well as wider is needed *J. chinensis pfitzeriana* will grow luxuriantly and make an impressive pile of feathered branches. *J. c. p aurea* has glints of gold in its green foliage and *J. c. p. glauca* has silver-grey leaves. All these will grow from 3 to 4 feet.

Taxus baccata repandens has dark bronze-green foliage and would be a good choice where dense colour is needed for contrast against lighter subjects. This prostrate yew has branches that curve gracefully at their tips and looks rather like a small dark creeping juniper.

The low-growing savin junipers are bushes with graceful feathery branches, some spreading horizontally, others growing at an angle which make them extremely useful for filling in corners and for using as ground cover against stone pedestals, steps or ornaments, or at the bottom of walls. Among the good dwarf varieties are Blue Danube, Grey Owl or Hicksii, with leaves of grey-green or blue-green. *J. chinensis pfitzeriana compacta* is a low, flat-topped and densely feathered bush. *J. Sabina tamariscifolia* is an attractive prostrate variety which is particularly good for covering banks.

The dwarf spruce, *Picea abies procumbens*, is a wide-spreading bush from $1\frac{1}{2}$ to $2\frac{1}{2}$ feet high with horizontal branches. In *P. pungens glauco-procumbens* the leaves are a bright glaucous blue.

A silver fir which grows sideways instead of up is *Abies procera (nobilis) glauca prostrata**. It is an open spreading bush, with blue foliage. It is not as thick as some conifers and though it covers the ground does not make very close ground cover; it also prefers a lime-free soil.

Perhaps the bright dwarf shrub *Thuya occidentalis* Rheingold is not everybody's idea of ground cover. It grows to $2\frac{1}{2}$ feet high but it is wider than its height and with its uneven growth gives the impression that it is crouching on the ground. It is a bright bronze-gold, so vivid at times that it is almost orange, and it seems to get even brighter in the winter.

~ 9 ~

Annuals for Ground Cover

Very pretty summer effects can be achieved by using annuals to cover ground that would otherwise be bare. Early flowering shrubs and plants are dull later in the year, but interest in the late season can be maintained by planting carpets of small plants which will soon join up to make a solid block of vegetation and will flower for weeks on end.

Such things as dwarf sweet peas (Cupid or Tom Thumb or Burpees Early Dwarf Bijou) will flower for a long time, the dwarf antirrhinums (Rock hybrids, Magic Carpet or Tom Thumb) are 9 inches tall only and make sturdy little shrubby plants, and tiny sweet Williams (*Dianthus barbatus* Wee Willie) are very suitable for the purpose.

We all have our favourite plants. Some people use ageratum which need not be only lavender-blue in colour but can now be grown in white or salmon-rose, as well as bright blue, *A. houstonianum* (*mexicanum**) Little Blue Star is bright blue and very compact. *Alyssum maritimum** (*Lobularia maritima*),sweet alyssum, is not only pretty in white but comes in lovely shades of lilac and purple. There is a deep rose variety called *A. m.* Rosie O'Day and a new pink, *A. m.* Pink Heather.

Nor need lobelias be in blue only. In addition to dark blue, bright Cambridge blue and white there are strains of *Lobelia erinus compacta* in wine and carmine-red, and a new mixture called String of Pearls in which all colours are included. No annual is better than lobelia for covering the space between big plants in flower beds and among shrubs. The plants grow all through the season and make a firm cushion of small leaves, covered with flowers which go on until frost intervenes.

Some annuals come up regularly year after year once they have been grown in a garden. I cannot remember when I grew *Limnanthes douglasii* by intention, certainly not for ten to fifteen years, and yet it still comes up regularly each year in sufficient quantities for me to replant it to make delightful sheets of glistening gold and cream against a background of light yellow-green finely cut foliage. One year I grew echium, and for several years thereafter I was able to repeat my carpet of blue, with pink tinges, from self-sown seedlings. Echium dwarf hybrids include shades of rose, lavender and blue and bring pleasant drifts of soft colours among plants that have finished flowering for the year.

Above: This dense cover features a competitive combination of the silver-splashed foliage of *Lamium galeobdolon* 'Florentinum' and the cream-flowered *Symphytum ibericum* with a self-sown plant of honesty, *Lunaria annua*, bravely holding its own. (East Lambrook Collection)

Above: Like its relatives *Anemone blanda* and *A. apennina*, the wild wood anemone, *A. nemerosa*, makes a delightful spring carpet in dappled shade. (Marianne Williams)

Overleaf: Despite its bold upright flower stems, the broad basal foliage of *Phlomis russelliana* makes excellent and effective dense ground cover. (Marianne Williams)

The delicate green spikes of *Tellima grandiflora* arise from a dense evergreen mound of prettily lobed leaves and the overwintering foliage of honesty also plays its part before these purple flowers appear. (East Lambrook Collection)

Above: The low foliage of *Veronica gentianoides* makes neat, well behaved cover and from it arises a long season of slender spikes. (East Lambrook Collection)

Below: The spreading roots of yellow loosestrife, *Lysimachia punctata*, make effective tall cover in moist soils but the plant is too vigorous for all but wilder areas. (East Lambrook Collection)

Right: *Sedum spectabile* is not a vigorous spreader but its tight clumps of glaucous foliage make dense cover. *Buddleja alternifolia* sweeps down from above. (East Lambrook Collection)

In moist conditions the summer snowflake, *Leucojum aestivum*, makes surprisingly dense ground cover and will also flower prolifically. (Marianne Williams)

The woolly, silvery-white rosettes of *Onopordum acanthium* can be more than 2ft/60cm across then, as enormous flowering stems develop, they reveal a different beauty. (East Lambrook Collection)

The low tight mounds of *Cotoneaster microphyllus,* whose arching branches are sprinkled with dainty white flowers in spring, are studded with red berries in the autumn.
(East Lambrook Collection)

The boldly cream-edged foliage of *Hebe x andersonii* 'Variegata' nestles against *Chamaecyparis lawsoniana* 'Fletcheri' on the terrace garden with the densely covered border behind. (East Lambrook Collection)

Having slowly built up its dense mass of foliage all summer, 'Sedum 'Herbstfreude', which Margery Fish knew as 'Autumn Joy', is one of the staples of the season's finale. (East Lambrook Collection)

Clumps of grape hyacinths emerge through the white-splashed foliage of *Lamium maculatum* 'Roseum', one of the prettiest of ground covers for light shade. (East Lambrook Collection)

Amongst the many ground covering violas at East Lambrook, 'Nellie Britton', sometimes known as 'Haslemere', is a lovely prolific lavender-rose with dainty streaks in the throat. (East Lambrook Collection)

In any soil that is not parched, *Lamium maculatum* 'Album' covers the ground well, is never invasive, and is especially effective in shade. (East Lambrook Collection)

Making dense clumps that are never invasive, *Actaea rubra* follows its spikes of dusty white flowers with these shimmery scarlet berries. (East Lambrook Collection)

Bergenias were amongst Margery Fish's favourite ground covering perennials, and especially this *Bergenia cordifolia* 'Purpurea', combining dark flowers with foliage that turns purple in winter. (East Lambrook Collection)

The dense planting on the sunny terraces ensures that weeds have little chance to develop and every inch of ground provides interest. (East Lambrook Collection)

The ditch garden is a particularly good home for hellebores like this prettily spotted form; their bold dense summer foliage is valuable when the flowers are over. (East Lambrook Collection)

Pulmonaria saccharata and its forms are amongst the most effective of all ground covers combining attractive evergreen spotted foliage with a flurry of blue flowers in spring. (East Lambrook Collection)

In sunny and well drained situations such as The Lido (behind the malthouse) at East Lambrook, *Euphorbia characias* subsp. *wulfenii* makes a dense and elegantly spreading evergreen plant that is always interesting. (East Lambrook Collection)

When in flower *Salvia officinalis* 'Purpurascens' combines blue spikes with dusty purple foliage and makes a dense shrub into which the pink pompoms of *Phuopsis stylosa* are starting to sprawl. (East Lambrook Collection)

Like other forms of the plant, this pale yellow form of *Iris foetidissima*, which Margery Fish referred to as the Chinese form, makes dense clumps of arching evergreen foliage. (East Lambrook Collection)

The elegant rich and glossy green foliage of *Hosta lancifolia* is followed in late summer by this airy display of lilac flowers. (East Lambrook Collection)

Many years ago I had *Silene pendula compacta* as an annual to cover some of my bare species, which it does well because it makes wide clumps by the end of the season and is very dwarf. The one I grew has bright pink flowers and I still find a few odd seedlings each year. It can be grown in white, pink and crimson.

The annual *Oxalis rosea* is a wonderful plant to make a cover of soft pink flowers under trees, and for many weeks *Polygonum capitatum* gives a rich-toned carpeting effect. This is a trailing plant with many heads of pink flowers against good foliage and reddish stems and the general picture is definitely sumptuous. Although strictly a tender perennial, it is best treated as an annual and raised each year from seed.

In places where a bright colour is appropriate I should use *Tagetes* Lemon Drop. It has double canary-yellow flowers which are large in proportion to its 9-inch stature, and they are produced right up to the time when autumn definitely gives place to winter. There are many other dwarf tagetes with flowers of primrose, yellow or orange, and they all make a fine colourful carpet for a long time.

Eschscholtzias can be grown in many attractive shades from cream to flame and the dwarf varieties make good cover plants. A very good strain for the purpose is *E. californica* Mission Bells, being dwarf and compact with large semi-double flowers well above the foliage.

It is safe to introduce annual convolvulus as a bedding plant and there are some good trailing and dwarf varieties which give colour and interest for a long period. They can be grown in various colours in shades of blue, lavender, crimson and tricolor. A particularly good variety for covering the ground is the rich royal blue tricolor Royal Marine.

We do not often think of mignonette these days, but this old-fashioned plant will make a very thick growth in the season as well as being sweetly scented. *Reseda odorata* is now available in several shades from white to red, with shades of yellow between.

I always like the colloquial name of Baby Blue Eyes for nemophila. This trailing plant is very good for massing, particularly *N. menziesii*, which is sky-blue, and *N. m. alba*, its white form. Another plant which makes a thick growth but is dwarf and neat is *Gypsophila muralis*, with rose flowers.

Dwarf zinnias are becoming more popular because they seem to produce many very large flowers for the size of the plant. *Z.* Red Riding Hood is a foot high and has brilliant double scarlet flowers, about an inch across, which smother the plants the whole summer. A new zinnia has made its appearance which would also be delightful for ground cover. *Z.* Thumbelina is something quite new in zinnias, never growing more than 6 inches high and starting to flower when only

4 inches. It makes bushy branching little plants with many leaves and many double and semi-double flowers. It keeps on blooming for three months and has flowers in white, yellow and orange, pink, lavender and scarlet.

It is not only for flowers that we grow annuals for ground cover. There are many exciting foliage plants that add greatly to the beauty of the garden and some of them are annuals. I always sow seeds of *Silybum marianum*, the milk thistle, which is also called Blessed, Holy, or Our Lady's Milk Thistle. There is a legend that the white stains on the large leaves were caused by the falling of a drop of the Virgin Mary's milk. The leaves of bright glistening green are handsomely cut and waved and cunningly barbed with scattered spines. The marbling and variegation are caused by broad white veins. If one is strong-minded enough the plant is not allowed to flower and then all its strength goes into the leaves, which will be finer and last longer. The flowers are quite handsome, violet thistles on 5-foot stems, but as they begin to grow the basal leaves deteriorate and the plant becomes tall, and monumental plant, not ground cover as one usually pictures it.

An ornamental basil, *Ocimum basilicum* Dark Opal, that has become very popular in America is gaining renown here, for its deep black-purple leaves are quite outstanding. It has flowers too, rather small and single and mauve in colour, and though they fit in very well with the picture it is not the purpose for which it is grown. The plant is not too tall for ground cover for it grows only to a height of 1½ feet, and as well as being colourful is strongly aromatic.

~ 10 ~
Ground Cover for Acid Soils

Of all the carpeters that must be grown without lime I think *Cornus canandensis* is the most effective. It is an unforgettable sight to see the regimented ranks of flat rosettes of leaves, all about the same height of 6 inches from the ground. The stems are so slender and yet they hold up their flat canopy of leaves so that they are absolutely level. In June a large white four-petalled flower (actually the 'petals' are bracts) opens on top of the leaves, and again the sight is unforgettable with the flat white flowers looking up into the trees above. When the flowers are over there will be a red berry in the middle of each rosette of leaves, and even then the display is not over, for the leaves themselves turn crimson and gold. When happy in light peaty soil this dwarf cornel runs about and spreads quite quickly. The only place I can grow it is in my peat garden and there it is undeterred by the big peat 'spits', working its way though them and emerging from the sides and top. It must not get too dry and I think it does best in shade, although I hear it will grow in sun, at a pinch.

I can see eyebrows being raised when I suggest shortias and schizocodons as ground cover plants, and yet the idea is not so fantastic, for in the right conditions they will spread as quickly as ordinary bugles do for me. The right conditions, of course, are moist soil completely free of lime and real shade. Both these plants should be grown where the sun cannot reach them. I do not think they mind if the soil is poor. In a woodland garden in Sevenoaks where the soil is light and sandy they make huge patches. In Mr Hadden's wood in West Porlock they grow luxuriantly at each side of the path, spreading into large clumps. I was as pleased as Punch when I got one of these little Japanese plants (it was *Schizocodon soldanelloides magnus*) to grow for me, and when it produced three little fringed pink flowers I was beside myself. To achieve this I planted it in greensand and arranged a stone to give it the shade it needed. When I admire it growing in large patches, as it does when it is happy, I realise that my poor efforts were quite artificial. *Shortia uniflora grandiflora*, to give it its full name, has shell-pink flowers' fringed, but not so thickly as schizocodons. Both have well-shaped glossy leaves which turn brilliant shades of crimson in the autumn.

It is probably asking for more criticism if I suggest *Epigaea repens* as a ground cover plant. But I do not think it is any more difficult than shortias – in the right conditions – and it is just as insistent on a cool lime-free soil as the two Japanese woodlanders. I have seen epigaea making a flat carpet under the shade of trees on a soil that was moist and mostly composed of rotted leaves. I grew epigaea for years in my peat garden. It was planted in the shade of a tall heath and spread itself out on a huge block of flaky peat. It died during a hot dry summer when it was impossible to give the peat garden all the water it needed.

While we were discussing the rather choosy plants for acid soils I had better include the pretty little trailing *Linnaea borealis*, often called the twin flower. This never makes very thick ground cover, but it is a dainty little plant for rather special places with shell-pink twin flowers and small leaves. It needs fairly damp woodland without a trace of lime.

Much more co-operative, *Dryas octopetala* really needs a lime-free soil, although it is not so insistent as some plants. I have grown it quite successfully several times in my ordinary limy soil, but it never lasts for very long. It will grow in sun or shade and is a good plant for covering a bank. The oak-shaped leaves are rather dark, and the white, golden centred flowers turn to balls of silky down and last like that for many weeks.

The dark shining leaves of *Galax aphylla** are rounded in shape and sometimes as wide as 3 inches across. They colour well in winter, especially those that have the fullest exposure to light. It is a plant for cool woodland conditions and produces slender spikes of white flowers about the end of June.

A dwarf iris may be an unusual suggestion for ground cover, but I have seen gardens on acid soil where the tiny *Iris lacustris* makes large colonies and with its strong underground roots is very efficient ground cover. It has taken possession of a trough of lime-free soil in my garden and its knotted roots discourage all weeds, so I think it could be used in special sunny places where something a little unusual is wanted. The flowers are pale blue and look like miniature flag irises.

When lithospermum gets the soil it likes it spreads very quickly and makes thick mats of dark green foliage and flowers on and off for months on end. For ordinary purposes *L. diffusum* (*prostratum*) Heavenly Blue is very co-operative and increases well. *L. d.* Grace Ward has larger flowers and they are a little brighter in colour, but I have not found it spreads so quickly as the more ordinary type.

Most of the ground cover plants that delight in an acid soil are shrubs. Many gaultherias make spreading plants and soon cover a large area. They really require very little attention when they are established, and do best in shade. One of my favourites is *G. cuneata*, which I grow in my peat garden. There it has not much room to spread, but it would revel in a wider scene and is easily increased by 2-inch cuttings taken in August and reared in a cold frame. This gaultheria is quite dwarf, and seldom grows as high as 12 inches. It has small leaves and reddish-brown stems. The long sprays of white lily-of-the-valley flowers are succeeded by large glistening white berries, which last many weeks.

G. procumbens is more prostrate, and never more than 6 inches in height. This is the well-known wintergreen, checker berry or teaberry of North America, and has small glossy leaves which turn crimson in autumn. The lily-of-the-valley flowers are tinged with pink and the red berries that come after are quaintly cut at the apex. Each plant can be guaranteed to cover a square yard and makes a close cover.

Another creeping gaultheria is G. nummularioides, which comes from the Himalayas and is a bare 6 inches above the ground. It makes long strands, with heart-shaped leaves edged with hairs, which decrease in size as the stems grow out. It does flower, but is so private about it that one has to look for the hanging dullish pink bell flowers under the branches. Sometimes they are followed by black berries. G. n. nummularifolia* has smaller leaves and makes a thicker growth, but seldom flowers so has no berries. The tiny G. n. minuta* is smaller altogether and has wiry creeping stems with reddish flowers in the leaf axils. It hugs the ground and each plant covers ground about 2 feet square instead of the square yard the other forms of this gaultheria will cover.

The most exuberant of the gaultherias is of course G. Shallon, which makes a close thicket and will do for acid soil what Hypericum calycinum does in limy soil. When there is a wide space to be filled nothing is better than G. Shallon, but it should not be introduced in a small area or where there are small plants that are liable to be overwhelmed. It is a steam roller of a plant and easier to put in than put out. It is a very attractive shrub with wide oval leaves in dark green. The sprays of white flowers are flushed with pink and the purple-black berries that follow them are said to be good to eat, but I have never tried them. When this gaultheria gets too untidy and rampant it can be scythed and will emerge in all the glory of fresh young growth.

Pernettyas are magnificent dwarf shrubs for lime-free soil, the best for ground cover being P. mucronata in its varying forms. The berries are more showy than the flowers, and where there is a good planting of pernettyas there will be no weeds. To get good berries one male plant should be grown with every three females. There are several good colour variations and the colour in this case refers to the berries. P. m. alba is, of course, white. Another good white with large and plentiful berries is P. m. Donard White. There are several pinks. P. m. Donard Pink is a soft shade. In P.m. lilacina and in rosea coccinea the pink has a mauve tinge. In P. m. rubra lilacina the colour is deep purple-rose, and Bell's

Seedling has large dark red berries. The colour of the berries in Davies' Hybrids ranges from white to deep purple. The average height of a good bush of pernettya is a little over 3 feet, and they grow wider every year, suckering as they go, in time covering a large area. With their dark evergreen leaves and cheerful berries all through the winter they are ground cover at its best.

The bilberries that grow on our moors make good ground cover and in cultivated soil would probably produce more and bigger berries. *Vaccinium myrtillus* is our wild bilberry, and *caespitosum* is the North American dwarf bilberry which is only 6 inches high. The cowberry also grows in wild parts of Britain and is also sold by some rock plant nurseries. *V. vitis-idaea minus* makes a good carpeter with pink flowers and red berries. The Cranberry, *V. oxycoccus*, is a dark green creeping plant, which grows in bogs and sphagnum moss but will do elsewhere. The bearberry is very similar to the cowberry and is also a good carpeter. *Arctosaphylos uva-ursi* makes long trails with blunt dark leaves. Waxy pink bells turn to red berries. Shade and acid sandy soil are the best way of pleasing this plant.

The bog rosemary, *Andromeda polifolia*, needs a damp position and is sometimes found in the wild growing with sphagnum moss. It does not ramp, but it makes clumps about 15 inches square, and has grey, rosemary-like foliage, and nodding waxy pink flowers shaped like tiny urns.

Two neat little evergreen shrubs that delight in an acid soil can be relied on to discourage weeds, although they are by no means rampers. *Ledum groenlandicum* makes a bush about 3 feet square, and has narrow scented leaves and terminal small white flowers. This is the Labrador Tea Plant and there is a compact form. *Leiophyllum buxifolium* is the sand myrtle, and makes a good evergreen shrub with small dark, shiny, box-like leaves with rose-red buds opening to starry white flowers. Again it is not a running plant but a small reliable shrub. The form *L. b. prostratum* is more dwarf and more spreading, making a bush 6 inches high and about 3 feet square.

The partridge berry is a pleasant little carpeting plant for a light peaty soil in semi-shade. *Mitchella repens* has small round leaves, which are dark green and shiny and are borne on wiry shoots which creep along the ground covering a patch about 2 feet square. The small pink flowers are bell-shaped and hang in pairs in the leaf axils and later turn to scarlet berries.

Bog myrtle, *Myrica gale*, is a bigger plant, growing from 2 to 4 feet in damp, lime-free soil. Sweet Gale is so called because it has a pleasant, slightly resinous fragrance. It grows in bogs and damp moorland in various parts of England and can make patches from 2 to 4 feet square. It is deciduous but has attractive red-brown twigs. The leaves are grey-green and the catkins are quite colourful.

Another lime-hating evergreen shrub which makes a mat of dark glossy leaves is *Leptarrhena amplexifolia* (*pyrolifolia*). About 9 inches high, it has clusters of purple flowers in spring and does best in shade.

Heathers are often recommended for ground cover and many of them are good labour-saving plants for covering the ground, giving colour for long periods and requiring little attention.

Very great care must be taken to see that the soil is absolutely clean before heather is planted, for if such weeds as running grass or ground elder get into clumps of heather it is a very difficult job to get rid of them without damaging the plants.

Some varieties are better than others for making dense carpets. One of the most satisfactory is the bright pink *Erica vegans* Mrs D. F. Maxwell, which makes a dense mat about 18 inches high and flowers in late summer. C. D. Eason is a form of *E. cinerea* and makes a tight, compact plant about 9 inches high and has luminous red flowers in June, which show up well against its dark foliage.

Among the callunas (*Calluna vulgaris*), Co. Wicklow* is a low growing silver-pink, H. E. Beale a magnificent double pink which grows to 1½ feet, and *serlei aurea** has golden foliage and white flowers. These heathers are late flowering, and are at their best in September and October.

The winter-flowering heathers are the carneas, which do not need an acid soil and so do not belong in this chapter.

Daboecias are, of course, allied to the ericas and have larger flowers which are more widely spaced so that the plants do not give as much colour as the heathers. But they do make dense spreading bushes about 18 inches high and flower from June onwards. *D. cantabrica* (*Menziesia polifolia*) has purple flowers, *D. c. alba** is of course white, and in *D. c. atropurpurea** they are crimson. *D. c. bicolor** has white, purple and parti-coloured flowers on the same plant, and *D. c.* Porter's Variety is a dwarf with crimson red flowers. *D. c. praegerae* is also dwarf and compact, being only about 9 inches, and has rosy-red flowers. For a sheltered, sunny position *D. azorica* makes a wide, low-growing shrub with glowing garnet flowers.

~ 11 ~

Evergreen Ground Cover

Very early in my gardening career I was taken to task by an experienced gardening cousin for giving too much space to perennial candytuft, *Iberis sempervirens*. When I first made my terraced garden I had the idea of having a tapestry of dwarf plants in different coloured leaves, and for this I felt that the very dark green foliage of *I. sempervirens* would show up other things, and being evergreen it would look well at all times of the year. I still like it very much, but I find myself curtailing its activities somewhat as I find more and more new plants I want to grow.

Iberis increases by underground stems and makes a very thick cover about 9 inches high. The best variety is *I. s.* Snowflake, which has large white flowers in spring which completely smother the plant. There are some dwarf forms as well; *I. saxatilis* is about 3 inches and after blooming for many weeks in the spring it continues on and off throughout the year. *I. sempervirens* Little Gem grows a little taller, usually about 6 inches, and *I. s. garrexiana* is 9 inches and particularly generous with its flowers.

At first glance *Waldsteinia ternate* (*trifolia*) might be taken for a cross between a buttercup and a strawberry. It seldom grows more than 3 inches high and a single plant soon covers a square foot of soil, as its fleshy roots stem as they creep along the ground. Its yellow flowers are like those of the strawberry and hang in clusters in early spring. It will grow anywhere and I have it doing well in both sun and shade, although it is usually recommended that it should be planted in shade. Another of its good qualities is willingness to do well in dry places, and so it is a very good plant for growing under trees.

At last people are again appreciating London Pride, *Saxifraga umbrosa*. It was a most popular plant in Victorian days and many an old garden still has large plantings covering awkward places in shade. I noticed the wide borders at Hardwicke Hall had large tracts of London Pride, and we could profit by this example. It makes an excellent ground cover for sun or shade, wide bands can divide beds from paths, and banks, odd corners and narrow beds under walls will never look bare or untidy if *S. umbrosa* is planted. Sometimes called St Patrick's Cabbage – and I do not know why – it increases by underground stems, and the rosettes of different sizes become enmeshed until they are one solid mat. In spring the plants can hardly be seen through a froth of filmy pink flowers, and in the autumn there are warm tints on the dark, encrusted leaves. In *S. geum* the leaves are much darker and turn even brighter crimson in the autumn. It can be used in the same was as *S. umbrosa* but does not increase quite so quickly.

Geums are evergreen and have good foliage, they also increase quite well. One of the neatest is *G. × borisii**, which has exceptionally dark leaves and orange flowers which, though bright, do not jar. The yellow flowers of *G. montanum* turn to balls of silken fluff, and even *G. rivale* Leonard's Var.* (the good form of our native water avens) makes good ground cover for a damp position as it increases well. The hanging heads of bronzed rose flowers keep opening throughout the summer.

Although such herbaceous potentillas as Roxana, Gibson's Scarlet and Miss Willmott grow from a central crown and have non-running roots, they produce innumerable long and leafy stems with flowers of brick red, scarlet and bright pink. These lusty stems spread themselves out in the soil and cover about a square yard of soil. The smaller *P. × tonguei* does the same thing on a smaller scale and soon makes quite a mat of foliage. Its flowers are apricot with crimson centres.

I have never been very successful with *Potentilla alba*, which has rather long, three-fingered leaves in pale green. It does not increase at all quickly and never looks very happy, although some people find it quite co-operative. So I stick to the more plebeian *P. montana*, which I have classed with trailing plants.

Violets do extremely well in my garden, almost too well I sometimes think, when I find their innumerable progeny coming up in every bed. But sometimes I am most grateful for those tracts of glossy leaves, later to be covered with scented violets in purple or white, pink, crimson or sulphur. I used to think that violets preferred to grow in shade, but I do not think they mind sun, because I find as many in full sun as I do under the shade of trees. Quite a number put themselves among herbaceous plants in the terrace garden. At one time they were all white, but lately I have noticed other varieties making their appearance, not in single plants but in large clumps which seen to grow overnight. I was pleased when I found a square yard of the little sulphur violet, in another place there is quite a big colony of the bright blue John Raddenbury. On my south facing rock gardens the little pink Coeur d'Alsace thrives, and in another place all the little strangers have crimson flowers. All these are forms of the sweet-scented *Viola odorata*.

More luxuriant foliage is provided by the white form of *V. Czar*, a long-stemmed variety, with bigger flowers. Ordinary mauve types appear occasionally, although I have never planted one in the garden. Then there is the red-purple L'Arne which is the French market violet; Admiral Avellan is a red-violet, and a pale blue-grey is well named French Grey. Sometimes I find great clumps of pale pink or bright cerise, and there are still descendants of the pinkish-mauve Corsican violet and the tiny white and green Christmas violet. Unfortunately the double violets do not increase fast, so do not make such good ground cover. Their foliage is a paler green, rather more glossy, and the leaves are smaller. Left to themselves the clumps do get bigger and send out a few runners, but they never thicken up and turn themselves into wide mats as the single violets do.

Nor do the large flowered violets make such good ground cover in spite of their thicker stems and bigger leaves. I have always had small plantings of Governor Herrick, Princess of Wales, Bournemouth Gem and the pink-centred Countess of Shaftesbury, but they do not increase much and never seem to seed themselves.

Veronica gentianoides has all the qualities most appreciated in a ground cover plant. It is evergreen, with glossy foliage, and very neat in growth. It increases well and makes a pleasant feature for the front of the border among autumn flowering plants. It produces tall spikes of pale blue in May and June which do not last very long. After they are cut back the dark foliage remains to show up the colours of the plants around. If there is time to lift and divide the plants regularly the rosettes are much bigger. I have a form with narrower pointed leaves and flowers of much darker blue, but have not a name for it. Some forms of the variegated *V. gentianoides* have deeper blue flowers. The leaves of this veronica are splashed with cream and sometimes flushed with pink, but I do not find it increases very fast and certainly does not thicken to a solid mat as the plain green one does.

Armeria maritima is a plant so tough and good tempered that it can be walked on without sulking. It increases fast and is easily increased because it can be pulled apart and each little piece will grow. Used in wide bands as an edging it can be kept in bounds with a sharp spade, but if something solid and quick growing is wanted to fill a corner or camouflage rough stones, this thrift is a reliable choice. The ordinary wild armeria has rather washy lavender-pink flowers, but there are several improved forms. *A. m.* Bloodstone has intense blood red flowers, in *A. m. laucheana* the flowers are crimson and there is one with white flowers. *A.* Corsica* is quite distinct. The foliage is much finer and the brick red flowers small and neat on slender stems. *A. caespitosa* is a much smaller plant and useful only for small areas. *A. c.* Bevan's Var.* and *A. c.* Six Hills have deep pink flowers, large in proportion to the plants. *A. plantaginea* makes large tufts and has big flowers on 18-inch stems but does not increase as quickly as the others, nor do I find that *A.* Bee's Ruby does, although the clumps themselves are large.

Several of the cardamines are evergreen and do particularly well in a position that is not too dry. Small and rather unobtrusive, *C. trifolia* has very dark, beautifully shaped leaves and small white flowers in dainty sprays. It does not ramp but it holds its own, and once in the garden it will stay. I always feel I ought to do more about it, and I am sure if I took trouble to increase it I should soon have enough to carpet many shady places.

A white cardamine that is on a bigger scale in every way is *C. asarifolia**. It is definitely anxious to oblige and soon fills big spaces between shrubs. It is about a foot in height and so is *C. latifolia**, a robust Lady's Smock with purple flowers. I have found the variegated cress a very tough little plant which has survived the intense cold of recent winters with admirable equanimity. The flowers can be ignored, except for the purpose of seed, but the gold and bright green of the leaves is cheerful.

In a shady, cool spot the pointed grey-green leaves of *Omphalodes cappadocica* are never untidy and the flowers of forget-me-not blue last a long time. This plant increases well but does not spread, divisions are soon big enough to cover a square foot of soil. The other easy omphalodes, *O. verna*, has running roots and takes a little time to make a thick carpet. The leaves are small, dark and hairy, and it has innocent blue flowers that give it its name of Blue-eyed Mary.

Another blue flower with good evergreen leaves is the rather rare perennial forget-me-not, *Myosotis dissitiflora*. It is easily distinguished from the ordinary forget-me-not, by the light colour and slightly glossy surface of the leaves. It sows itself quite well in my garden and I plant the seedlings to make ground cover round trees in my mixed borders and to fill the space between perennials. This forget-me-not has larger, more open flowers than the bedding plant, and they always remind me of the guileless flowers of Blue-eyed Mary.

In gardens where it is happy *Campanula persicifolia* is quite good as a ground cover plant. I often find quite large plants in places where I certainly have not planted it. It increases with small white roots, like many other campanulas, and makes a thick cover of dark pointed leaves. The flowers come and go for most of the summer and those open cup-shaped flowers in white or blue are graceful on their slender stems. I have had named varieties, but so much intermarrying goes on that I am now content with the hostages of nature. I pay more attention to the cup-and-saucer types, and when some of the seedlings have this type of flower they are carefully marked. I find plenty of white but have one only in blue and a washy blue at that. Some of the white forms have touches of green, which add to their attraction. The double forms of *C. persicifolia* have never settled down with me, but who minds when the lovely single ones are so obliging.

For years I have grown a low, fleshy erigeron which I was given as *E. glaucus*, and nothing could make better ground cover for a bank or wall. It has greyish leaves and by the end of the season will be covering about a square yard with its dense foliage. The flowers are large and flat and can be pink or mauve. There is a wild form that has rather dull and washy flowers and is found on cliffs in Dorset. The neat *E. Elstead Rose* might be a miniature form of this daisy; that too spreads and has glaucous foliage, but it is a smaller, neater plant than my unruly daisy.

Both forms of *Arabis albida** make shaggy ground cover and may have to be cut back by the end of the season. The ordinary single white arabis can be nothing more than a weed, but it is useful for very rough places. The double white arabis is a much more attractive plant. It can be rather straggling and is not such a neat growing plant as the single form, but its flowers, like scentless double white stocks, are much more attractive. Aubrietias will soon cover the soil if they are planted a foot apart and are a good idea for a bank that needs covering. Being evergreen they look nice all through the year, particularly if they are cut to the ground after flowering.

*Geranium sanguineum lancastriense**, the refined form of our native bloody crane's bill, was found on the island of Walney, off the coast of Lancashire, and has all the good qualities of that indefatigable plant and none of its vices. It thickens but does not run, burrow or delve. Its leaves take on the same brilliant tints of crimson and gold in the autumn, it produces its flowers over a long period, and in this case they are pale pink veined with crimson. A small plant will cover a square foot of soil before the season is out and what is more will have something to offer throughout the year.

Stachys macrantha does not make such a close clump but covers the soil quite pleasantly with dark and hairy leaves, which are deeply veined. Though each plant covers only 9 inches square it does this most thoroughly and the plant is capable of very rapid increase, for each small piece with its shaggy roots grows quickly into a good plant. It makes a pleasant contrast to gold or silver plants and I have used it successfully with the rose Frau Dagmar Hastrup, the orchid flowers of the stachys blending with the soft pink of the rose.

All the epimediums grow well in shade and have beautiful leaves. Some are more evergreen than others, so make good ground cover. Probably the best for ground cover is *E. pinnatum*, with soft yellow flowers. It is strong growing and spreading. In *E. p. colchicum** the yellow flowers are dark centred. *E. perralderianum* is also good for ground cover. It has particularly good yellow flowers and glossy, toothed leaves which turn chestnut and crimson in autumn. Anyone who has had dealings with epimediums know what solid, interlocking roots they have; they make a solid barrier against all weeds and when one wants to increase them they can be divided into many small pieces, each of which will root. In the National Trust garden, Tintinhull in Somerset, broad bands of *E. pinnatum colchicum** are used to border the beds in the courtyard nearest the house. Though in full sun the plant does extremely well and is esteemed for its flowers as well as the leaves. In early spring the late Mrs Phyllis Reiss cut off all the leaves so that only the flowers made a show, and the plant looked so different treated in this way that many asked what it was. It is usually recommended that the old leaves are left on the plants until the flowers are over, for in low lying gardens the flowers can be damaged by frost, but the plants at Tintinhull suffered no inconvenience by the removal of the leaves and got thicker and denser every year.

A lime-free or neutral soil is needed for the prostrate *Lithospermum diffusum* (*prostratum*). It has very dark leaves and makes a large dense mat many feet square. *L. d.* Heavenly Blue is the ordinary form and its intense blue flowers come and go for most of the year. *L. d.* Grace Ward has larger flowers and there is an uncommon form, *L.d. album*, which has white flowers with a blue tinge. There is a rampant lithospermum for wild shady places which does not mind lime, *L. purpureocaeruleum* will grow in dry chalky soil, in fact it can be used where nothing else will grow. This is another plant used at Tintinhull. Behind the spreading branches of *Cotoneaster horizontalis* at the far ending of the pool garden this lithospermum is an effective dark carpet, with inky blue flowers. It has an extended manner of growth, sending out long stems (sometimes about 3 feet) which root where they touch the soil and make small tufted plants, which in turn start a long-arm movement. Very soon there is a tangle of arching stems studded with blue flowers. The plant needs plenty of room and is definitely not desirable for a normal rock garden.

Prunellas make neat carpet plants if they are kept trimmed, but if the dead heads are left on the plants soon look dishevelled. The biggest is *P. grandiflora*, with violet flowers on foot high stems. A recent introduction of a soft pale blue form called Loveliness has put prunellas on the map. Before they were not of much count, but this well-named beauty is worthy of any place in the garden. The flowers are bigger than the ordinary forms of *webbiana* and there is also a lovely pink shade and a white. There are two with deep pink flowers. The rich deep pink is sold as a form of *P. grandiflora*, and a crimson, *P.incisa rubra*, has deeply cut leaves and rich crimson flowers. The prunellas spread and can be easily propagated by taking off small rooted pieces. I have found that they sometimes get a little threadbare and need dividing or top-dressing with good soil. Do they revert, I wonder, to their wild state? If not, how is it that plants of the ordinary wilding, with its ordinary blue flowers, keep popping up in the vicinity of named varieties? At first glance it may deceive, but the leaves are small, the plant more dwarf, although it has the same rather dark green leaves. When it flowers, of course the game is up.

Some primulas have neat foliage, and being evergreen they look well all through the year. On the whole I think the smaller polyanthus are best for the purpose. Most of the primroses have leaves that are longer and more lax and they get untidy. But the leaves of such polyanthus as Old Rose, The Bride, and the dwarf pink Kinlough Beauty, which has rather prostrate rooting stems, are neater. Polyanthus with purple foliage makes a good contrast. Any of the Garryarde primulas has this lovely foliage and so has the dwarf, crinkled Wisley Red, which is neat and low-growing and has crimson flowers.

Also most effective, if it is a plant that likes you, is *Gentiana accaulis*, which makes solid neat carpets of glossy bright green leaves. It may increase well even if it does not flower, and those tight cushions are splendid to fill the ground between other plants or make wide bands of evergreen foliage.

I get considerable pleasure from the rich brown leaves of *Polygonum affine* in the winter time. This plant makes wide mats on beds, pathways, or among stones, it is quite good tempered and will grow in sun or shade, but yet is a plant capable of high positions in the planting world. There have been several improved forms, especially the form collected by Lowndes. I first saw it on the rock garden at Kew and admired the very fine colour of the thick, sturdy flower spikes. *P. a.* Darjeeling Red is said to be better than the normal type but it is disappointing when it first starts to flower. The later flowers are deeper in colour but not as solid as the Lowndes version. I notice that some of my plants are better than others and I think those with the deepest flowers are growing in more shade than the others.

While *P. affine* is undoubtedly good for giving us rich brown leathery leaves all through the winter, another low growing polygonum does the same thing with green leaves, leaves that sometimes turn crimson in winter but for the most part remain green. *P. emodii* has very long, narrow leaves, greyish-green in colour and with conspicuous veins. It has a habit that I can describe only as sideways. My only complaint is that it is mean about its flowers. These 3-inch spikes of blood-red flowers are rather thin when they do appear and they are not produced nearly so generously as those of *P. affine*; nor in the case of *P. vacciniifolium* either, for that matter. This busy little plant flowers profusely and, like the others, late in the year. From the ground cover point of view it is particularly good where it can drape a bank, cascade over rocks, or just quietly potter along among stones, filling each crevice with sprays of small, glossy leaves, which you may have guessed are like a vaccinium. It puts down roots where it touches, and its leaves have good autumn tints, so it is an admirable little plant for steady increase, but could never be called a ramper. From August to October it will be covered with 6-inch spikes of soft pink flowers and is really a memorable sight. To see it at its best I recommend the rock garden at Kew, where it smothers some of the largest stones, or working its way down among the stones in the rock garden at the National Trust garden, Killerton, in Devonshire. This rock garden is on the side of a hill. It is not what we would make today, but represents a period and is therefore interesting. I was glad to see the polygonum because not much else except the larger trees and shrubs had survived and it was nice to know that this little knot-weed would not let go where frailer subjects gave up.

Ground Cover for Sun

It always surprises me that the creeping Dutchman's Pipe, *Aristolochia sempervirens*, likes to grow in full sun. With its dark green heart-shaped leaves, twisting slender stems and curious purple hooded flowers, it looks just the plant to hide away in a cool leafy spot, but it is not as tough as it looks and likes to bask in a warm position.

Another rather surprising plant that does best in full sun is *Eriogonum umbellatum*, a good evergreen carpeter which produces yellow flowers all through the summer. This plant from the Rocky Mountains needs a light sandy soil: it makes a thick mat of leaves about 6 inches high, with the umbels of yellow flowers rising above it.

The Greek bedstraw, *Galium olympicum*, with its white flowers, is a small plant for a sunny scree, but our native *G. verum*, lady's bedstraw, is an easy plant to please and in a sunny place produces clouds of tiny greeny-yellow flowers which are very pleasing. I saw it used at the top of a sunny wall in a famous garden with great success, but I had no idea what it was and had to ask. I would never have thought of bringing in this modest little plant, but it has a featheriness and lightness that contrasts well with more solid plants and it is pleased to come in.

Rosemaries and cistuses are used to basking in the sun and they are excellent for clothing hot dry places, since they usually grow rather informally and are inclined to sprawl, particularly the ordinary rosemaries. Unfortunately they are not completely hardy, but if planted in poor soil, are more likely to survive a very hard winter.

It is a pity that the prostrate rosemaries, which are the best for low ground cover, are usually even less hardy than the big rosemaries, but there is a hardy Spanish form of *Rosmarinus lavandulaceus* (*R. officinalis prostrates*) which is good for hot dry places. It has low arching but wide spreading branches, lavender flowers and fresh green leaves.

For ground cover the more prostrate types of cistus are the best to use, and if the soft shoots are continually pinched out it encourages them to branch.

Cistus × *lusitanicus decumbens** (*C. loretii**) has large white flowers with brown spots. *C. corbariensis** is one of the hardiest and is also low growing. It has fresh green waved leaves and white flowers which are yellow at the base. With a height of 3 feet it will spread to 6 to 9 feet. *C.* Warley Rose* is even lower in growth, and has dark sage green leaves and bright pink flowers.

Spanish gorse, *Genista hispanica*, is tough and sturdy; it likes the sun and is long-lived. Seldom more than 2 feet in height, a single plant can spread to 5 to 8 feet in time and makes solid and reliable ground cover.

Most silver plants do best in full sun and poor soil and the santolinas are no exception. *S. chamaecyparissus* (*S. incana*) can make a neat rounded bush or a spreading mound according to the way it is pruned. I always cut mine down almost to the ground in spring and a crop of new young growth very soon covers the maimed stems. *S. c. nana* is a good compact form, useful for many spaces. Cuttings root very easily and small plants put in a foot apart each way soon join up to make a solid block of frosty foliage. For a bigger space the more feathery *S. neapolitana* is a good plant to choose. It will grow tall if allowed to, but can be kept fairly low by judicious cutting. Both these santolinas have small button flowers of bright yellow. In some cases they fit in with the scheme, but sometimes it is better to cut them off and keep the silver foliage without ornament.

The green santolinas like the same conditions as the silver ones, and they too can be cut hard back in the spring so that they make firm mounds of bright green foliage. I grow *S. pinnata* with lemon flowers.

Dwarf lavenders can be used and these can be kept low and spreading if they are trimmed immediately after flowering. Great care must be taken never to cut into the old wood. One of the best for making a wide bushy mound is *Lavandula* Twickle Purple. It is rather taller than some and usually grows to about 2 feet, but as the tall spikes of dark purple flowers fan out instead of rising vertically it covers more space, and a single bush can soon fill a space almost a yard square.

L. Folgate Purple is a low-growing variety with soft lavender flowers and silver-grey foliage. Its height is about a foot and it covers about 2 feet of space. For heavy scent I would choose Backhouse Purple and for depth of colour in the flowers Hidcote Purple, a variety which combines silvery foliage with very dark flowers. A new variety, *L.* Gwendolen Anley, blooms later than the others and has flowers of pinky lavender. Its average height is 1½ foot.

Smaller plants that make excellent ground cover in full sun include all the hieraciums. *H. aurantiacum* is too invasive for any but very wild places, but the silver ones are ideal, especially the running *H. pilosella* which sends out long stems with silver tufts at the ends, each of which makes a small new plant, with primrose hawkweed flowers. It is evergreen, as is *aurantiacum*, with its orange flowers, but *H. waldsteinii, H. villosum* and *H. lanatum* are not. These are easily raised from seed, and with their wide leaves covered in white woolly down soon grow into good clumps and meet each other to give a solid cover of glistening foliage. These plants range in height from 1½ foot for *H. waldsteinii* to 6 inches for *H. lanatum*.

Veronica incana has spreading capabilities and it makes a good cover of silver leaves with deep blue flowers on foot high stems. In *V. i.* Wendy the flowers are violet-blue and grow a little taller.

Though *Oxalis floribunda* is reduced to a bundle of rhizomes in the winter, it is covered with flowers and foliage all through the rest of the year, starting its season in spring and not closing down until frosts spoil its shamrock leaves and translucent stems. Sometimes a white seedling appears among the bright pink ones and makes a variation in the endless succession of bright pink flowers that open whenever the sun is shining.

Sedums enjoy a hot dry position and there are many from which to choose. A new one called Ruby Glow is a good one to choose, as it is not too dwarf and spreads quickly. It is a cross between *S. cauticola* and Autumn Joy and has lush purplish-grey foliage about 9 inches high. It produces its glowing ruby-red flowers between August and October, but even without them gives a colourful and luxuriant effect.

~ 13 ~
Instead of Grass

Although we do not often hear of it described in that way, grass is, of course, the best ground cover plant there is. Lawns are nothing but superlative examples of ground cover on a big scale, to be walked on and to act as a background for the gay colours of the flowers we grow. There are gardens without any grass, for sometimes it is impossible to keep it cut and trimmed, and then it is better to design a garden without it, for badly kept grass is far worse than no grass at all. I often think such gardens lose a great deal of their beauty and restfulness, for good grass is one of the most beautiful things in the world and it helps to make a garden beautiful.

Sometimes the absence of grass is due to inaccessibility and the difficulty of getting a mower up precipices or down steep slopes. Or the places concerned may be too small to be cut easily. And there are gardeners who can do anything else in the garden, plant, weed and trim, but not use a mowing machine, and then a substitute for grass is a good idea, but only for small areas and then not for heavy traffic.

In a terraced garden on a steep slope it is restful to have a few patches of green but impracticable to have grass. A large rock garden needs the relief of green amid stone, scree and chippings. I often think as I scrape the annual arenaria off the beds that it would make a good green carpet, and *Sagina subulata* does. The golden form, *S. subulata aurea*, also thickens up well and a small golden lawn is pleasant for a change. *Arenaria balearica* makes a really dense carpet of bright green and I notice that weeds do not grow through it. It must be started in a moist, shady place and so long as it does not get too dry it spreads in all directions and makes a very firm, close carpet. It would not mind an occasional footfall but would probably not stand up to heavy traffic. *Cotula squalida**, on the other hand, is very tough and its green ferny foliage has a bronze tinge.

I have to stop *Mentha pulegium* from encroaching on adjacent flower beds and creeping up into the lawn, when it is intended for it merely to wander at will in paving cracks. When it gets the chance to take hold of a nice piece of soil it makes a dense, fragrant mat, which will stand up to a lot of wear. It needs shearing after flowering but practically no other attention, for the growth is very tight and solid. Just as *M. pulegium* is working its way among the grass of the lawn in one place, *M. requienii* is doing the same in another, and being much smaller its presence is received with more enthusiasm. Though so tiny the little plants have flat green leaves which will soon spread and cover the surface of the soil, and in summer there are microscopic lavender flowers. It seems to want to get out of the sun and is most luxuriant where the ground is slightly moist, and then lumps of soil with their film of green can be carved out and planted elsewhere. It has the strongest scent of peppermint of any plant in the garden, and I always thought it was a stroke of genius on the part of the late Victoria Sackville-West to fill the open centre of a stone seat with it. But she found that her visitors did more than brush the fragrant chair seat with their hands – too many little pieces came away for it to be accidental, and I do not recommend this kind of planting in a garden open regularly to the public.

I noticed *Pratia treadwellii* trying to oust the grass in a lawn in Ireland. But there the grass is very green and luxuriant and the pratia was not winning, but in another garden on sandy soil it had no competition and the interlocking stems were weaving themselves into a dense mat, with tiny flat leaves along each side of the stems, perky white flowers, like little lobelias, and later purple berries. *P. repens* is even better for the purpose as it is smaller and makes a mat of closer texture.

Creeping thymes, if left to themselves, make really strong carpets and will cover any given space. In a garden I know the rectangular spaces between a stone path and surrounding flower beds are thickly covered with creeping thymes. As well as flowers in white, pink and crimson the different shades of foliage make a pleasing mixture. There are different scents as well, the astringent smell of pines from *Thymus caespititius* (*T. azoricus*), caraway from *T. herba-barona*, and suggestions of lemon, geranium and lavender from others.

The Curse of Corsica, as *Helxine soleirolii* is sometimes called, will fill any available space that is damp and shady with a sponge of fine green, but it is too delicate for traffic and a hard frost turns its tender leaves to blackened pulp. It increases at a great rate and invades every crack, cranny and empty space it can find, and in a place where it can be contained there is nothing better for covering dark corners, spaces in courtyards and gaps under walls. It would make a small lawn in a dark damp place but could not be relied on for big areas.

Chamomile lawns are quite practical, particularly on a light sandy soil, and are an excellent idea for covering a bed where small bulbs, such as crocus and scillas, are grown. A large clump of chamomile (*Anthemis nobilis**) can be broken into many pieces and these planted in sandy soil soon take hold, because each stem is shaggy with roots. After a while the planting may become a little leggy and then a top-dressing of sand and peat will help. Most people prefer the double flowered to the single form for such a purpose and the cutting off of the flower stems after flowering is all the attention it needs.

A chamomile which does not flower, and is therefore particularly good for chamomile lawns, has been developed by Miss Dorothy Sewart of Treneague. She calls it *Anthemis nobilis* Treneague and understands that 'it originated from a lawn in one of the royal residences'. In Miss Sewart's experience this new chamomile does best in lime-free soil, which makes one wonder if all the chamomiles prefer an acid soil. I grow both the single and double-flowered forms on my very limy soil, and have never experienced any difficulty with them.

I had never seen moss used as a carpet until I visited a garden made in a wood. Small gardens, like separate rooms, had been made by clearing the scrub, leaving an evergreen framework. Lilies made ideal subjects to grow against the dark background and the natural moss on the ground had been allowed to grow and thicken. This dark, velvety carpet kept perfectly so long as it had shade and was kept clear of fallen leaves. Brushing with a stiff brush from time to time kept the moss lawns in good trim.

~ 14 ~
Roses as Ground Cover

There are some roses that make excellent ground cover, but it cannot be stressed too strongly that where roses are to be used the ground must be absolutely clean. Once the roses are there it would be extremely difficult to get out perennial weeds such as couch grass, ground elder and bindweed, to say nothing about the damage to hands and clothes. Roses should be thick enough to avoid danger from above in the form of seeds from annual weeds, and there are several that make most attractive and unusual ground cover.

One way of using them is to peg down the long trails of hybrid perpetual roses. Sometimes this is done among taller roses, but that seems to be gilding the lily and I should prefer to divide my riches by using the ground cover roses round early flowering trees and shrubs that grow in the open, such as *Prunus subhirtella autumnalis* and spring-flowering magnolias. Many of these roses flower better when pegged down. When grown in an upright position the flowers come at the end of stems only. The stems must be trained closely enough to make a dense carpet.

The large white rose Frau Karl Druschki is very effective grown this way, and when the many flowers are at ground level the absence of scent is not so disappointing. It says much for this old rose that we are still buying it more than sixty years after it was introduced. It is strong and blooms for a long time, and though the flowers are pure white the buds have a pink tinge and when the flowers open they reveal a lemon tinge in the centre.

Mrs John Laing is an even older rose and it still has many followers. Its large double pink flowers are produced generously. There is a lilac flush in the pink of the flowers and the foliage, though plentiful, is not dark and shiny as is often found in good ground cover roses, but its soft green, with a dull smooth surface, is very pleasing.

There are two hybrid perpetuals named after the Dickson brothers, Hugh and George. George Dickson is not a good rose for ground cover as it is inclined to hang its head, but the vigorous Hugh, with bright scarlet-crimson flowers, is ideal, and when pegged down produces flowers all along its well-clothed stems instead of merely at the end of the stem. Souvenir d'Alphonse Lavallée is another rose which produces flowers all along its stem when it is pegged close to the soil. The blooms themselves are not very big but they are very shapely and of velvety texture in an intense shade of dark crimson which has no trace of purple. This rose needs a good soil if it is to do its best.

Not quite so easy and needing to be planted out of the sun, Souvenir du Docteur Jamain has dark velvety flowers, but they are of a purplish-crimson and liable to be burnt by very hot sunshine. It has the advantage of flowering a second time in the autumn and deserves a good soil.

The flowers of Baron Girod de l'Ain are rather like those of Roger Lambelin, in deep crimson with a white deckle edge. But it has a more robust constitution and though it misses the elusive attraction of Roger Lambelin it is far easier to please, and looks as though it enjoyed life, which the other seldom does. Its leaves are broad and handsome, it flowers for some weeks and has a minor second display in autumn.

There are still people faithful to such old friends as American Pillar and Dorothy Perkins and these are both easy to train along the ground. But our tastes are changing and I for one would prefer the pastel pink New Dawn, which is very robust and extremely prolific, or Albéric Barbier with creamy-white flowers and the very popular Albertine with its copper-pink flowers. Both these have good glossy foliage and so has the silver-pink Dr van Fleet and the deeper pink François Juranville, which adds brilliant red shoots to its attractions. Sander's White is a good white rambler, with rather small flowers and dark shiny leaves.

There are several roses that can be used for ground cover without any assistance from the gardener. *R. wichuraiana* grows very close to the ground and makes a close carpet of small shiny leaves, spangled with tiny pale cream flowers. It will do quite well on a light, sandy soil and can be admired in the R.H.S. gardens at Wisley when it blooms in August.

The usual conception of ground cover is something flat and carpeting, but if I had a large space in a border which I wanted covered for permanent beauty I would plant the rugosa rose, Frau Dagmar Hastrup. It has everything to recommend it – good dark foliage, a wide and spreading habit and plenty of large single flowers in a delicious shade of pink that has not a trace of blue. Conspicuous cream stamens are a feature of this rose. It flowers twice and its second blooming is often made more spectacular by the large crimson fruits, which ripen about the same time. They have been likened to small tomatoes, but their colour is richer and deeper and has a soft bloom to enhance their beauty. This rose is sometimes used for hedges and it will also furnish a trouble-free narrow border against a wall, for no weeds could possibly raise their heads under its canopy of green.

R. Schneelicht is another rugosa that can be regarded as good ground cover. It makes a wide spreading plant with arching stems studded with yellow-stamened white flowers. Eventually it may reach a height of 5 feet but by then it will probably be twice as wide.

Several of the rugosa hybrids have the same useful qualities, particularly *R.* Max Graf, which is a cross between *R. rugosa* and *R. wichuraiana* and has the good qualities of both sides of the family. It has trailing branches, seldom more than 2 feet high, which makes a dense cover, for they root as they go and cover everything in sight. The flowers are single pink with a few extra petals, white centres and golden stamens.

R. paulii (*R. rugosa repens alba*) is equipped with most venomous thorns, which would make it good ground cover without its dense trailing stems. The flowers are white, with conspicuous yellow stamens, and the bracts which are typical of all rugosa roses are particularly noticeable perhaps because of their pale shade of green.

Some of the sprawling roses cover plenty of space between larger shrubs and trees and can be regarded as ground cover because they certainly swamp anything that comes in their way. *R.* × *macrantha* can be used for covering a bank and here its tangle of arching stems shows off to the best advantage. It has flowers of warm pink which fade to near white. *R.* × *m.* Daisy Hill has better flowers, which are slightly double and *R.* × *m.* Raubritter has flowers that are even more double and rather rounded in shape. Reaching 3 feet eventually it spreads its long arms in all directions, and they are laden with flowers even down to the lowest branches.

Weeds do not grow among a small planting I have of *R. nitida*, so I think this might be considered suitable for filling in between shrubs that are fairly dwarf. The rose itself seldom grows higher than 12 to 18 inches and it colonises well, thrusting up its sturdy, thorny stems in a miniature forest. It has pink flowers, red hips and leaves that turn brilliant crimson in autumn.

There are, no doubt, other roses which can be used. America is producing carpeting roses, but so far I do not think they are available in this country nor do we know how effective they will be as ground cover.

~ 15 ~

Trailing Plants

Many of the plants that we are used to seeing trained to fences and walls can be grown horizontally just as well as vertically. When I have struggled to discipline the strong stems of *Clematis davidiana**, heavy with handsome leaves and clusters of Wedgwood blue flowers, I have often thought how much easier it would be to lease the bonds and let these luxuriant stems tumble about together on the ground. Other herbaceous clematis can be used in the same way. Although *c. jouiniana** has smaller flowers than *C. davidiana* it makes a great deal of growth and the heavy ruffled stems would make effective ground cover. *C. jouiniana praecox** flowers two or three weeks before *C. jouiniana*.

The everlasting pea, *Lathyrus latifolius*, is quite happy if it is planted under a tree and encouraged to make an unruly swirl of coarse leafy stems and clusters of crimson or white flowers. It is grown in this way at the National Trust garden, Tintinhull, in Somerset and looks delightful tumbling about under a massive cedar and providing adequate and unusual cover.

I have never tried hop, *Humulus lupulus*, as ground cover, but it grows so strongly that I imagine it would grow horizontally if it was not offered an upright support.

Akebia quinata has very well-shaped leaves and chocolate-purple flowers and this too can be denied support and encouraged to cover the ground. Dutchman's Pipe (*Aristolochia macrophylla*) has large and handsome leaves and curious green and purple flowers.

The climbing hydrangea, *H. petiolaris*, is not evergreen, but it will provide large and handsome horizontal foliage with large cream heads of flower. In a sheltered spot *Coronilla glauca** will furnish the ground attractively with blue-green leaves and yellow pea flowers in winter. The more rampant *Coronilla varia* will grow anywhere and has pretty pink and white flowers.

Some of the honeysuckles can be used in this way, particularly the easily grown types. *Lonicera henryi* is a vigorous plant with dark green glossy foliage and rather small reddish flowers. The golden veined leaves of *L. japonica aureo-reticulata* show up well on the ground, and when *L. j. halliana* is used there are many sweetly scented cream flowers for a long time in the second half of the year.

There are several members of the rubus family that make good ground cover, but all except the variegated blackberry and *R. fockeanus*, which are not rampageous, need a wide scene because they are robust in every meaning of the word. I have never measured the furry brown stems of R. *tricolor*, but some of them must run into many yards. The leaves are dark and glossy and there are sometimes edible berries rather like those of the Japanese wine berry, but never on mine. This plant does best in shade and is a plant for the milder counties. *R. flagelliflorus* is even more rampant. It has very handsome large and evergreen leaves, heart-shaped and covered underneath with yellowish felt. The stems of the plant are slender and almost white. The double pink blackberry, *R. ulmifolius bellidiflorus*, is not a carpeter because its long trailing stems fountain from a central crown and make a low arch when the ends are pushed in the soil where they soon root. This plant will keep out weeds from above but will not smother weeds already in the ground, so it must be planted in clean soil. The stems are rich crimson and the small leaves dark and glossy. When the stems are smothered with little mauve-pink roses the effect is delightful.

Brambles lead us to vines, and some are good when a large area has to be covered. *Vitis coignetiae* has enormous leaves sometimes 12 inches across, which turn wonderful shades of orange and crimson in the autumn if the soil pleases them. This vine is often used for covering old tree stumps and is a good plant where good cover is needed for rough uneven ground. I have heard of gardeners using Virginia creeper, *Parthenocissus quinquefolia*, and *P. inconstans*, but I have never grown them in this way. I do use the variegated form *P. henryana* as ground cover in the shade of shrubs. The soft blending of cream, pink and pale green is very pleasing, but it does not grow very quickly and is not satisfactory for large areas.

Geranium traversii Russell Prichard* has trailing stems of well-shaped silver foliage, against which the magenta-pink flowers do not look too gaudy. Two evening primroses have long and well-furnished stems which will cover the ground. The foliage of *Oenothera missouriensis* (*O. macrocarpa*) is the most effective, the large flowers are pale yellow and are followed by very big seed pods. *O. acaulis* (*taraxicifolia*) is so named because its leaves are the shape of dandelion leaves. It too has long trailing stems which lie flat on the ground, with large flowers at the leaf axils. Though the flowers start white they end up pink and then large fleshy seed pods adorn the stems and last for many weeks.

The trailing *Potentilla montana* is one of the most satisfactory ground cover plants I know. It is neat and evergreen, it is a conscientious worker but by no means an overbearing rambler, and it attaches its stems to the soil as it goes so that it makes a solid carpet. Its small white flowers are produced throughout the year, in fact I have never known a day when there were not a few of them to be seen.

The various forms of *Vinca minor* make the most effective ground cover as they grow flat on the ground, sending down roots as they go. New stems branch out in all directions until there is a criss-cross of stems and leaves with flowers at the ends of the shoots in spring. The common form of *V. minor* has blue flowers, and so has *V. m.* La Grave or Graveana, which is one the late E. A. Bowles found and which is sometimes called Mr Bowles' vinca. It has larger, deeper coloured flowers and a more compact form of growth. It will grow in the sun, and if treated like a violet and all the runners cut off will make a solid clump covered with flowers. The double form, *V. m. caeuruleo-plena* is not completely double but very pretty with crumpled petals growing where the stamens should be, but not so thick that the delicate markings inside the flower are hidden. There is another double blue vinca called *V. m.* Celestial, supposedly better in colour but I never see much difference.

I know three forms of white *V. minor*. The ordinary white is, of course, the counterpart of *V. minor* and has flowers about the same size. Then there is Mr Bowles' pet white form, which has larger, more solid flowers, delicately flushed on the outside, and dark rubbery leaves. Miss Jekyll's form* is quite different with smaller, almost transparent, pure white flowers and markedly smaller leaves. It grows differently too, making a definite clump from which it sends out stray stems.

The flowers of *V. m. rubra* (sometimes called *V. m.* Burgundy or *V. m. punicea*) are more wine-coloured than red, and they vary from a faded claret to a richer shade nearer port. The double form of this, *V. m. multiplex*, is less double even than the double blue, and at the beginning of its flowering is often single. Later it has one or two extra petals, like bits of crumpled silk pushed into the centre of the flower, as in the case of the double blue.

Gardeners are discovering that many of the small 'fancy' ivies are hardier than it is sometimes assumed. Small variegated ivies, generally seen as house plants, have proved quite hardy in my garden and survived one of the worst winters ever known. Whenever I go to a function where house plants are given as presents to the ladies I inevitably choose a variegated ivy, and just as inevitably I plant the ivy as ground cover the moment I get home. The only cheerful things in my garden one awful winter were the variegated ivies, and that year Somerset was as hard hit as anywhere. When everything else was frozen to ramrods, desiccated by intense cold and seared by unceasing bitter winds, the ivies remained sleek and untouched. There was no green leaf of any kind to pick except ivies, and I filled the low bowls which suit my heavy oak tables with sprigs of ivy – trails of the frilled 'parsley' ivy, *Hedera helix cristata**, with its warm tones in winter, and snippets of small variegated ivies.

When the snow went at last the ivies I use to cover the ground under trees and on banks were just as good as before the winter and it has persuaded me that small ivies are excellent plants to recommend as ground cover.

One of the most cheerful of the little ivies, and one of my greatest standbys in winter is *H. h.* Jubilee Gold Heart*. It was given to me as plain Jubilee, but I understand that for purposes of identification it is better to refer to it by the longer name. For those who do not know it has red stems and very dark leaves, the centre of each being bright gold. Some leaves are all gold and are cherished, just as the occasional all green leaf is removed at once. As well as being tough it is generous in the speed at which it gets away from cuttings, sending long trails over the ground in all directions (or dashing up walls) and tending to be more liberally laced with gold the more shady the position in which it finds itself.

With me the most generous of the small silver variegated ivies is one of those given to me as a house plant, *H. h.* Harold, which I think is an improved form of variegated *H. h.* Chicago* and has bigger leaves, more constant in shape and colouring. A little less distinct in its variegations and with a broader leaf, *H. h. marmorata** is very co-operative and excellent for ground cover as it grows very quickly. *H. h. maculata** grows quickly too, but I do not think its speckled leaves made such attractive contrast as the cleaner markings on such a plant as *H. h.* Silver Queen*, which has beautifully variegated leaves and makes very long trails, which are not very closely clothed with leaves and not very quick to increase. I use it among dwarf shrubs and tall perennials where it wanders about without making very dense cover. It is inclined to be tinged with pink in winter, but has not the definite colouring of *H. h. marginata rubra** (*tricolor*), with its beautiful mixture of cream, pale green and pink, and is, I think, one of the most beautiful of the small variegated ivies. It is not a fast worker and for ground cover must be given the smaller, more conspicuous places in the garden, with such other treasures as *H. h.* Heise, an imported plant with very delicate colouring and congested leafy growth. Other charmers for these favoured positions are the variegated form of *H. h. sagittaefolia**, with its refined shape and pleasant habit of developing pink tints when it gets into the sun, and *H. h. elegantissima**, which has more solid leaves, crinkled at the edges and tending to take on a pink tinge round the outside of the leaves when grown in sun, and stems that are always grey-green. And even that is not the end of them, for there is *H. h. variegata minor, H. h.* Little Diamond, *H. h.* Iceberg, Fantasia, and *H. h. sub-marginata*, which has a fine pink and white line round the leaves. The small margined form sold as Silver Border is probably the same. A rather curious ivy I grow is *Hedera helix* Lutzii*; it is mottled in patches, sometimes half a leaf may be completely plain green.

For large spaces the delicate silver and white Glacier is good. It increases fast, and though its silver leaves do not stand out as brilliantly as the white variegated forms they merge softly into the undergrowth and tone with everything. Nearly all these ivies are very happy to be used as ground cover. Several of them that I started up a wall have slipped to the ground and are busy carpeting the soil instead of covering the wall.

There do not seem to be as many small golden ivies in general cultivation as silver variegated ones. One called Buttercup is, I think, the same as *H. h. Chicago* aurea*, and it is also sometimes called Gold Cloud and Russell's Gold. It is the same shape as Chicago and I do not find it at all easy to increase, in fact there have been times when I have nearly lost it. It is one of the golden leaved plants which does best in shade, and I have seen it grown very effectively among stones in a shady rock garden. But even this one is not always golden. In spring the leaves are lime green, they are golden in summer and often fade to green in winter. The other golden one I grow, *H. h. angularis aurea**, is not at all stable in colour and constantly reverts to green, although there are usually many golden leaves on the plant.

It always hurts me when I have to pull out ordinary ivy from the garden. It is really a beautiful plant with perfect leaves and one of the best ground cover plants we have, but it grows too easily in most English gardens. And left to itself it would swamp everything and produce forests of seedlings. I have seen it used as perfect ground cover filling in the ground at the edges of paths in churchyards and in other strictly controlled places, but it has to be kept carefully trimmed and supervised.

When I want a medium-sized ivy with green leaves and a pleasant disposition I use *H. h. cristata**, the parsley ivy. I planted it at the bottom of a wall and when it had climbed to the top, stray stems at the bottom worked their way across the bed and covered all the ground under a shrub. In another place it covered the sides of a frame and climbed over the wall behind it, then filled up all the empty spaces between frames and path with fresh green frilled leaves, many of which turn bronze and crimson in winter.

There are at least three tiny green-leaved ivies which very quickly make a smother of small well-cut leaves and are useful to cover ground under trees, disguise unsightly objects and work their way down banks. *H. h. sagittaefolia** has the most elegant leaves of all, long, beautifully cut and well described by its name. *H. h. feastii** is not unlike it, but the individual leaves are irregular and one-sided although the general effect is good. I find the third, *H.Nielson**, the most energetic. It has small dark leaves, not so narrow or pointed as the others, and produces many tiny leaves – about an eighth the size – among the larger ones.

The medium-sized green ivies being sold today are *H. h.* Green Ripple, with jagged pointed entire leaves which incline to grow on top of each other; *H. h.* Curly Locks*, which has dark green leaves frilled at the edges, and *H.*

*chrysocarpa** (*H. poetica**) Italian Ivy, which is, I think, synonymous with *H. helix* Emerald Green* or *lucida**, and has bright green leaves, often the older leaves turn bright copper coloured in winter, with green veinings.

Sometimes called Mr Bowles' Shield Ivy, *H. h. deltoidea** is quite distinct in its blunt triangular shape, with overlapping lobes at the base. The leathery leaves are blackish green and change in autumn to a sombre purplish bronze. It is sometimes sold as *H. purpurea*, but this is a separate species and, according to the late Shirley Hibberd, whose monograph on ivies is a standard work on the subject, *H. purpurea** is a purple, thick-leaved ivy, 'a fine purple-leaved variety of *coriacea**; the autumnal colour is sombre bronzy-purple, mottled with dull green, the principal veins being of a reddish colour'.

There are different versions of *H. helix pedata*, which is not surprising as it is occasionally found growing wild in Welsh woods. This is a five-lobed ivy with the central lobe exaggeratedly long and narrow and the side lobes narrow but shorter. With a stretch of the imagination it could be likened to a bird's foot. I have a greyish green version, given to me by a friend, called *H. h. pedata* Grey Arrow*, and another particularly straight and narrow version called *H. h. pedata* Heron*.

*H. h. caenwoodiana** is not unlike a small version of *H. pedata* and some experts hold that it is synonymous with *H. h. minima**.

The Irish ivy, *H. hibernica*, has large, bright green leaves and is very popular when something easy and attractive is wanted for covering quickly large bare tracts of ground, or walls. Why it is called *H. hibernica* is not very clear. I understand that it has been found growing wild in Ireland, but it is not by any means plentiful and its other name of *H. grandifolia** is probably more authentic.

The little congested ivies, *H. congesta** and *H. h. conglomerata**, are not really good ground cover plants unless one has really large specimens or uses a number of small plants together. They are neat and interesting, with their tiny dark leaves growing tightly together, and though I have seen big specimens swarming up boulders and making thick ruffled ground cover it takes some time for them to get as big as that.

The two large variegated ivies most usually grown are *H. colchica dentate variegata** and *H. canariensis variegata**, which is usually represented by *H. c.* Gloire de Marengo. This is the more beautiful of the two but it is not the hardiest, and in fact in a very hard winter leaves in an exposed position will be blackened and drooping although the plant itself is not dead, and ground cover specimens which are sheltered will be more presentable. It makes lovely ground cover for sheltered places, for the large leaves are an engaging mixture of ivory, grey-green and darker green, irregularly marked and often with a pink flush in winter. The variegated form of *H. colchica* is less subtle, but it is a very pleasant sight in winter with large leaves splashed with deep cream which looks almost like pale yellow in the winter. This ivy seems quite hardy and with its large leaves is useful for open spaces where something really spectacular is needed in the dark days.

~ 16 ~
Ground Cover for Roses

Not everyone will agree that rose beds look better if given ground cover. The ardent rose grower, with exhibiting in mind, would be horrified at the idea, and the owners of formal rose gardens, with humped beds, round a statue or sundial, would not allow anything to defile the well-forked soil.

But for most of us roses are not so sacred, we plant them in mixed borders, and many of us feel that without underplanting a rose garden is rather dull for the many months when there are no flowers. It may be argued that roses, being hearty feeders, need all the nourishment they can get. But I am sure that they are not deprived by the surface rooters I shall recommend for the purpose. I know my own roses are most happy as they flower above a carpet of small self-sown seedlings, which conserve moisture as well as adding to the beauty of the garden.

By degrees I am ousting the ordinary forget-me-not from the garden for the more perennial *Myosotis dissitiflora*, which seeds as well as the commoner. I now find that it is putting itself among roses, and I hope it will continue to do so. It has pointed, rather shiny leaves in paler green than the ordinary type, and larger, more open flowers, which have an even more innocent expression than the others. In May claytonia is a wonderful sight, foot-high clumps of fresh green foliage covered with delicate pink or white flowers. It does seed itself rather too much, but the roots barely penetrate the soil so that they take little out and are easily removed. Rather smaller than the other two, *Viola labradorica* has taken a fancy to the rose bed and chains of purple leaves weave their way through the forget-me-nots and claytonia. I can forgive the violet for not having scent, for the beauty of its evergreen purple leaves which go so well with its blue flowers.

I did plant the double-flowered chamomile, *Anthemis nobilis fl. pl**, near the edge of the bed, where it meets a stone path, because I wanted to get this plant going and thought a piece put in the safety of the rose bed would soon increase. It has and I now have a good patch, which also works its way over the stone path. Nearby the position is reversed and *Mentha pulegium*, pennyroyal, which is growing in cracks in the path, is working its way into the rose bed. I think both these subjects would be quite a good idea to plant near the edge of rose beds.

Before the rose bed was taken over by seedlings I used to find it useful for things I wanted to plant out; the well-enriched soil was just asking to be planted. One year it was carpeted with *Artemisia pedemontana*, and that thrived in the good soil. Another time it was *Chrysanthemum haradjani* that needed a temporary home, and small plants of that soon increased to wide clumps.

Seedlings of the dwarf *Lychnis flos-jovis*, with its bright pink flowers, had to be put somewhere until they were old enough to fend for themselves and they too looked remarkably well among the roses.

The soft woolly leaves of *Stachys lanata* make a pleasant background for roses and the plant takes very little from the soil as it is shallow rooting. But it would look untidy if it were allowed to throw up its 2-foot flower spikes, so they have to be kept cut, which, of course means work. There is a form which does not flower and I am using that for under-planting the roses and using the flowering version in other places.

Although I do not like to see my roses growing out of bare earth, I do not think one should use too rampant a carpeter. The ordinary *Ajuga reptans* does make rather a big clump and in a good soil would be a little too luxuriant. But the other bugles are not so rampant and the white-flowered bugle, in particular, makes a neat, rather bronzed close cover with short spikes of white flowers. The crimson leaved bugle, *A. reptans rubra*, spreads itself like so many gigantic star fishes under the rose trees, and the variegated form never gets very big although working over the good soil of the rose bed it does better than in most places. Though *A. genevensis* does not send out long stems it increases from its central crown and makes large clumps of neat, bright blue spikes of flowers. None of the bugles root deeply, so they are good plants to choose.

Although its mauve flowers are very welcome in the winter I do not want to see *Lamium maculatum* flowering its head off under roses in the summer. Then the mauve flowers are not so attractive and one wants them only under hedges and on outside banks. But the form with clear salmon-pink flowers is lovely always and goes with most roses. The white-flowered form also makes a pleasant background for roses. My answer to most ground cover problems is *L. galeobdolon variegatum* and when it is not in flower the long trains of silver and grey are beautiful anywhere, but I would not use it on rose beds because when it flowers the flower stalks would be altogether too overpowering for the dwarf rose bushes.

Some gardeners like *Vinca minor*, particularly neat varieties such as *V. m.* Miss Jekyll's Form, or the deep blue La Grave, but I do not think they quite suit roses; nor would I use heathers, which I have also seen used for that purpose. The small acaenas are better on a path, but of the two larger ones, Mr Bowles' Form with black stems and very blue leaves is neat and yet gives sufficient colour to be effective. *Acaena adscendens** is bigger and needs a fairly big bed if it is to do itself justice. It makes swirls of glaucous blue foliage and is very graceful in the way it grows. It would be a good plant for such tall-growing roses as President Hoover, which can look rather leggy.

Although violets are supposed to like shade and I would always plant them in shade, I find that many of them sow themselves in full sun and the seedlings seem just as happy growing in the sun, so it would seem suitable to underplant with any of the varieties of *Viola odorata*. Of course violets get rather leafy after they have finished flowering, but they flower very early in the year before the roses have started and then their flowers of pink, violet, blue, sulphur and crimson are very welcome. A pretty little white and green violet, given to me as the Christmas Violet or Skim Milk, is very fond of putting its seedlings in the sun. It is rather smaller than some and very pleasant as a background for roses.

Violas, of course, have long been admitted to rose gardens and they are good subjects, although they do need to be dead-headed if they are to go on flowering and if the rose beds are not to look untidy. I should not use *V. cornuta* or *V. c. alba* because it grows a little taller than the others and if it finds itself under a bush likes to work up among the branches, but this viola is ideal among old roses, which need a thick underplanting. In rose beds some of the winter-flowering violas, Helios, Ice King, Jupiter or March Beauty would be a good choice. The pale Moonlight also flowers in the winter.

I do not know how dedicated rose growers would take to the idea, but I was enchanted one cold morning early in the year to visit a garden where the rose beds were sheets of bright blue from squills, *Scilla sibirica*. My friend told me that her mother had planted them many years before and they had been increasing ever since without apparent harm to the roses. Small grape hyacinths, chionodoxas and puschkinias could be used in the same way and one could also plant *Anemone blanda* or *apennina* which disappear completely after flowering and do not seem to affect the beds in which they grow. Some of these bulbs and corms would probably be better grown at the edge of the bed, and the bright flowers of St Brigid anemones* would be cheerful as a border in early spring.

It was at Gravetye, the late William Robinson's famous garden, I understand, that low plants were allowed to soften the edges of rose gardens, and the idea is used at Bodnant, the National Trust Garden in North Wales, with very great success. It is a particularly good idea when the rose beds have stone paths round them, because the plants can be set very close to the path so that they fall over the edge of the path as well as on the rose bed. This may not appeal to the houseproud type of gardener who makes neatness a fetish, but it has a softening effect for those of us who do not like hard lines.

The smaller campanulas, *C. portenschlagiana* and *C. poscharskyana*, are good plants to use. They have evergreen foliage and go on flowering for most of the summer. *C. poscharskyana* is rather shaggy and might be a little exuberant in a small garden as it makes trails sometimes 18 inches long. This is a good place to grow rock roses which will not get out of hand if the dead flowers are sheared off after they have finished flowering, and dianthus like Musgrave, and Inglescombe*, the old laced and painted types. *Phuopsis stylosa* is inclined to seed itself about and has to be watched, but if kept under control can be very pretty with its thick ruffle of bright green foliage and pink flowers. There are two forms, one has rather dull, pale pink flowers which look dingy beside the deep pink form.

In a big rose garden I should use one or two of the prostrate oenotheras near the edge of the bed. They send out long stems from a central crown which do not root but lie about on the surface of the ground and make a barrier against weeds. *O. missouriensis* has quite large leaves and pale yellow flowers; *O. acaulis* (*taraxicifolia*), with leaves like those of a dandelion, also makes long trails with pale yellow flowers along the stems.

London Pride, *Saxifraga umbrosa*, is a useful plant for growing at the edges of rose beds, or in the beds themselves for that matter. In the winter *S. u. geum* would be good because it turns bright crimson, also the golden variegated form, with its flecks of gold and tinges of pink.

Double daisies are neat little plants which cover the ground with bright glossy leaves and are not greedy. There are several interesting ones in addition to the well-known daisies, Dresden China and Rob Roy, but all need constant division and good soil if they are to survive. The ground under roses is good for the purpose and it is where I put divisions of *Bellis prolifera*, the hen and chickens daisy, and others not too easy to keep. *B.* Bon Accord has large pink flowers, Alice (if you can find her) is a pink version of Rob Roy, and the Pearl, the white counterpart of Dresden China; all need good soil and regular attention if they are to survive.

Many of the daisies that can be grown from seed each year and treated as annuals make very pretty edgings; ageratum, alyssum and lobelias all make excellent ground cover in the summer and are often used, although it is in winter and early spring that I think colour and interest are needed. The gay little plants of nemesia, clarkias, dwarf godetias and even heliotrope detract from rather than add to the beauty of the roses; it is necessary to be very careful with colours and really a good background of green is best.

But primulas of the *juliae* type will bloom well before the roses, and I have often used my rose beds for planting out divisions of the salmon pink E. R. Janes, purple Jill, cream Lady Greer and pink Kinlough Beauty. There is enough shade from the roses to keep them from fainting in the summer and the good soil helps them to make good plants.

When it comes to underplanting shrub roses there is scope for much bigger plants and some of the more rampant plants, such as *Lamium galeobdolon variegatum*, which is too luxuriant for hybrid tea roses, would be excellent, for the ankles of these old tea roses are often bare and a flurry of light foliage and flower would give them a more furnished look.

Some of the geraniums are good too, *G. endressii*, particularly the form Wargrave* which has flowers of a more delicate shade of pink and a taller, more leafy manner of growth. The tall blue *G. ibericum** and the more dwarf *G. atlanticum** would go with pale pink roses, and *G. renardii*, with grey-green velvety leaves and pale grey flowers would be pleasant with various shades of old rose. *G. reflexum* and *G. punctatum** are very leafy plants and their small lilac flowers are not important enough to detract from the roses. *G. nodosum*, with its shiny leaves and lilac flowers, is just the right type.

One of the best plants for growing with old roses is, of course, the hosta, and it has all types of foliage to go with the different roses, glaucous, light or dark green, variegated or margined. Forms with the biggest leaves look best, *H. sieboldiana robusta, fortunei* and *ventricosa*.

In one garden I know where old roses are grown extensively, often three or four together in small beds, euphorbias are used at their feet. The most successful are the large types, *E. wulfenii**, *characias* and *sibthorpii**, and they were very successful with the roses, but after the wholesale slaughter in recent exceptionally cold winters I have second thoughts about recommending them. But it is quite safe to suggest *E. Robbiae**, which does not succumb to cold, *E. amygdaloides* and *E. hyberna*, which are all big enough to make an impression and have good foliage as well as beautiful love-bird green flowers.

~ 17 ~
Shrubs for Ground Cover

The number of shrubs that make good ground cover is quite large, but they will not all be included in this chapter. Some are mentioned among plants that ramp, others come among the plants with different coloured foliage, and there are many that need an acid soil and are included in that chapter.

Shrubs for ground cover can be roughly divided into two groups. First there are the flowering shrubs, although for ground cover they are grown more for their dwarf spreading habit than their flowers. *Potentilla fruticosa arbuscula* is a case in point. For though it has delightful sulphur yellow flowers from May to October and light green leaves, it is because it is the most dense of the *fruticosa* potentillas, and has a spreading habit, that we grow it for ground cover. Though only 2 to 3 feet high it will make a bush 4 to 5 feet wide, and young plants should be planted 2 feet apart.

Two good daphnes to grow are *D*. Somerset* and *D. burkwoodii*; both make leafy hummocks covered with sweetly scented small pink flowers. Roughly they grow to about 2 feet and are about 3 feet in width.

Skimmias are good value, for they offer lush evergreen leaves, sweetly scented flowers and large red berries which persist a long time. It used to be necessary to plant male and female plants together if one was to be certain of berries, but this has disadvantages when a good solid mass of foliage is wanted, because male and female plants do not always grow evenly. My lady skimmia, *S. japonica*, is about six times as big as her husband and I am grateful I am not growing them for ground cover. The hermaphrodite *S. foremanii* gets round this problem very nicely and as it has a spreading, bushy habit it is ideal for a shady position. Average size is 3 feet by 5 feet and the plants should have 2 feet between them. There is a theory that skimmias do best in acid soil, but mine thrive in lime.

Though *Forsythia* Arnold's Dwarf comes in the category of flowering shrubs, I have always found it rather mean with its flowers, and the flowers themselves are rather mean compared with other varieties of this shrub. But the dwarf makes a neat bushy shrub, with good leaves for the greater part of the year, and as it makes roots wherever its branches touch the soil, as well as from the tip of every shoot, it is quite easy to build up a flourishing colony.

The brooms and their close relatives make good ground cover because the slender stems grow so quickly that a dense brush is formed. *Cytisus kewensis* likes to be absolutely flat and makes a good ground cover plant between taller subjects. I grow it beside a big dome of purple sage with a large clump of diorama on the other side, and when the sheet of deep cream flowers is replaced by a tangle of green twigs the effect is still good. Seldom more than a foot high, it will eventually have a span of 6 feet. *C. procumbens* needs even greater care in placing because its flowers are bright yellow. The mat of tangled stems will cover 6 square feet in time and is composed of whip-like shoots. *C. × beanii* has somewhat the same colouring but is semi-prostrate only, being about 18 inches in height.

The most prostrate of the genistas is *G. sagittalis*, which has broadly winged prostrate branches with sprays of bright yellow flowers at their tips. It is about 9 inches high and makes a clump 1½ feet square. *G. pilosa* is also low growing, with small hairy leaves and has scattered yellow flowers. Although it will cover an area 2 feet across it is 6 inches high only and justifies itself for inclusion by a thick forest of arching slender stems, attractively green after the yellow flowers are over.

The ramping *Hypericum calycinum* had to be put in the chapter with the other rampers, but there are others that do not ramp at all. Two shrubby St John's Worts are striking because they produce flowers and berries at the same time. In *H. androsaemum* the berries turn from red to black, and in *H. elatum* Elstead Var. the fruit are scarlet. Both make useful wide bushes about 2 to 3 feet high. *H. buckleyi* is a neat little bush from America, not very common in this country. Its dimensions are 1 foot by 1 foot and its compactness does not extend to its flowers, which are an inch across.

H. moserianum is usually seen in its attractive three-coloured garb, for *H. m. tricolor* has lovely variegations of cream, green and pink. The green-leaved form is beautiful too and has pleasant green leaves. It makes a compact bush 1½ by 2 feet, and pays for careful pruning that will produce new basal shoots.

Hypericum rhodopeum Sunspot is a new prostrate hypericum highly recommended by Richard W. Lightly of Longwood Gardens, Pennsylvania. It arose in a batch of seedlings raised at the Plant Breeding Department, Cornell University. It has an even spreading habit, blue-green leaves and inch-wide bright yellow flowers, produced with great freedom.

The polygonums are borderline rampers. *P. reynoutria*, which is classed as a herbaceous plant but acts like a shrub, can be a problem in the wrong place, but where there is plenty of room it is a great success. It makes a bushy plant about 2 feet high with stiff stems that branch at right angles. Its leaves are long and narrow and it has myriads of small pink-flushed white flowers. Though it runs – and in my garden it dives under the fence and comes up smiling in the next orchard – it is not difficult to control. A sharp spade will sever its roots when they need curtailing, and each scrap will make a new plant. *P. campanulatum* (also herbaceous) blooms a little later than *P. reynoutria*, usually about August. It is not so invasive either, making a flat cover of long grey-green leaves from which the 3-foot stems arrive. The flowers are pale pink and quite pretty. In fact we should be very fond of the polygonums if they did not wander so much. The ordinary *P. cuspidatum* can be described only as a holy terror, and once it gets into the garden it requires strength of will as well as strength of arm, not to mention great perseverance, to get rid of it. *P. c. compactum* is not as bad as the type, but it does run and it should not be planted among civilised plants. It is pretty when the small greenish flowers turn to flat pink seeds, rather like the seeds of sorrel. I was once at Kew when the plants were dripping with their harvest of pink fruits and they were a wonderful sight. Because *P. baldschuanicum* is such an overpowering ramper the Japanese Fleece Flowers are not always appreciated as much as they might be, but properly controlled they can be most useful – and attractive.

In the second group of shrubs for ground cover I would put those that are particularly good because of their leaves. At the top of the list, of course, is *Mahonia aquifolium*, sometimes known as the Oregon Grape, because its fruits, with their heavy violet bloom, look like miniature grapes. The name gives a clue to the shape of the leaves, which are shaped and prickled like those of holly. The young leaves are almost crimson in colour, they turn to dark green before they take on their winter tones of maroon and purple. The bright yellow flowers open after those of *M. japonica*, and though they have not the delicious scent of *M. japonica* they are pleasantly robust. This mahonia is usually about 3 feet high and has a 3-foot spread. The form *M. a. undulata* has beautifully waved leaves but it grows to about 6 feet and is not so good for ground cover. *M. a. atropurpurea*, on the other hand, which has richly coloured leaves, is only 3 feet. *M. aquifolium* is particularly useful for any sunless spot; it grows well under trees, and its glossy, colourful leaves help the beauty of the winter garden.

Another mahonia that makes good ground cover is *M. nervosa*. This is by no means a common plant, it is neater in growth than *M. aquifolium* and its 2-foot stems are straight and stiff. The leaves are 18 inches long and a delicate green, often shaded with crimson when very young. It spreads by means of underground stems and though slow to establish is very co-operative when once it takes hold.

The creeping berberis, *M. repens*, is a low growing shrub, about a foot high and covering an area 4 feet square. It has bright yellow flowers, black fruit, which are heavily powdered, and colours in a quiet way in autumn. It takes a little time to settle down.

For many years I grew a single plant of *Viburnum davidii* for the beauty of its large, deeply ribbed leaves, some of which are 6 inches long, and for the shallow growth of the shrub, which makes it useful for ground cover. I enjoyed the leaves and felt it was a pity that such architectural splendour should have such indifferent flowers. The flowers are dull, but if male and female plants are grown together they produce clusters of bright turquoise berries as vivid as anything in the garden. Though this shrub is seldom more than 2 feet from the ground its span can easily be 4 to 5 feet.

There are two types of euonymus. Those that we grow for their berries are deciduous and make big bushes or small trees, so are not ground cover plants, but the evergreen types are perfect for the job. *E. radicans** is usually seen in one of its variegated forms, but it is attractive too when the leaves are green, running over the surface of a bed or bank, seldom flowering but giving good protection from weeds. *E. r. coloratus** is a more glamorous version, with leaves lined with dark red and tinted veins, and is particularly colourful in the winter. All these spindles are 3 inches only and should be planted a foot apart. The miniature of the family, *E. r. minimus**, is an inch high only and has tiny leaves. It is sometimes known as *E. r. kewensis**.

An aromatic sumach, *Rhus aromatica* (*R. canadensis*), is often used in American gardens to make a dwarf bushy shrub about 4 feet high. It has yellowish flowers followed by red berries, but it is the leaves that are aromatic and they also supply good autumn colour in tones of flame and crimson. It should be planted 18 inches apart and to keep it compact needs to be cut to the ground every few years. An evergreen ribes, *R. laurifolium*, supplies large leathery leaves, which are coarsely toothed and pointed, and drooping sprays of greenish white flowers. It is not a very fast grower but a good choice to grow under taller shrubs close to the house. It is usually about 3 feet tall and makes a clump with the same width.

A prickly subject but one that makes a dense clump is dwarf gorse. There are two varieties that can be used. *Ulex minor* (*U. nanus*) is usually about a foot high and makes a clump 3 feet square; it produces its golden flowers in late summer. *U. gallii humilis* is even more dwarf, being about 8 inches in height and making a spread of 3 feet square. The flowers are small in proportion and it, like *U. minor*, likes a hot, dry position.

Hebe (*Veronica*) *catarractae** is not often seen and I often wonder why. It is a neat evergreen plant with small dark green leaves. About 8 inches high, it has a very mild tendency to increase by underground stems. The flowers are small and star-like, usually white with a deep pink centre, although I have seen them in pale lavender-pink. The small shrubs should be planted a foot apart.

Another veronica that makes wonderful ground cover in light shade is *H. subalpina*. It is a spreading rounded bushy plant in brilliant green and most effective in winter. The leaves are oval and arranged very neatly, and the flowers are white. Average height of the plant is 2 feet with a width of about 4 feet.

The cotoneasters do their carpeting chiefly by stems. Anyone who has visited Dartington Hall, at Totnes, knows the large bank covered with *C. dammeri*. It is completely flat with glossy evergreen leaves about the size of privet. Because of its sturdy stems it makes a dense cover and to help the good work every new shoot should be pegged down with wire until it roots. It should be planted 2 feet apart. *C. adpressa* is not dissimilar, but it is deciduous and tends to make longer trails, and is therefore not so dense, although it grows close to the ground. Its pinkish-white flowers turn to very bright red berries, growing in ones and twos. The leaves colour brightly before they fall. In *C. congesta procumbens** the small evergreen leaves and small pink flowers are crowded together. Seldom more than 6 inches from the ground, it grows very slowly and is better in a small area. The berries are sealing-wax red, and each plant should make a mat about 2 feet square.

C. conspicua makes a spreading bush about a foot high and covering about 5 feet square. Its graceful stems look best arching in a bank or over a wall. The leaves are as small as thyme and the large white flowers become orange-red berries, which last most of the winter. The plants should be planted 2½ feet to 3 feet apart.

C. horizontalis is the best for growing on sunless banks or to give a permanent clothed look in beds against house walls. It does not hug the ground as some of the others do, but the large fan-shaped branches are so densely filigreed with stout stems that they smother all weeds. Nor is it evergreen, but those many-fingered branches never seem bare. Before the small leaves disappear they become crimson and then the plentiful red berries carry on. The variegated form grows more slowly and loses its berries more quickly, but it is lovely as ground cover with touches of pale green and pink on its silvered leaves. *C. Sabrina** is a hybrid of *C. horizontalis*, which is bushier in growth and its stems are more thickly studded with orange-scarlet fruit. These cotoneasters should be planted 4 to 5 feet apart.

Both *C. microphylla* and *C. lacteal* are usually grown as wall shrubs, but they can be made to run and root if the stems are pegged down. Both make excellent cover for banks. *C. microphylla* has small shiny leaves and *C. lacteal* long evergreen leaves in grey-green lined with white. It bears its flowers and then its bright berries in hanging clusters.

*C. hybrida pendula** will weep if grown as a small tree, but it can be trained flat. It is practically evergreen and keeps its berries till January. *C. Autumn Fire** has large leaves and has flexible spreading stems which make a flat carpet which will soon grow to 6 feet across. *C. integerrima* Arnold Forster* made cover for huge granite boulders in its Cornish home, but it has no objection to growing on the ground instead of stones.

Green-leaved shrubs make a good background for other plants. Though the two green santolinas have flowers, deep yellow in the case of *Santolina virens* (*S. viridis*) and lemon-yellow in *S. pinnata*, it is the all-the-year-round beauty of its green foliage that makes it such a joy in the garden. Like all the santolinas it grows very informally but this one makes a bush about 2½ to 3 feet for its height of 1 foot.

An evergreen honeysuckle, *Lonicera pileata*, makes excellent ground cover and I find it most attractive for underplanting tall shrubs and massive perennials. When shrubs are bare and perennials die down there is the thick growth of bright green narrow leaves on horizontal branches. With me it seldom gets more than a foot off the ground and makes flat clumps about 4 to 5 feet square. This honeysuckle does flower, a little more than our hedging *L. nitida*, which of course never gets a chance with its constant clipping, but not very extensively. The flowers are cream, narrow and well stamened and come spitting out of the branches at leaf axils. They are scented, but not very heavily, and should later become translucent purple-violet berries, but do not do this for me often. After a bad winter and heavy snow which can reduce other honeysuckles to blackened wrecks, the low-growing *L. pileata* emerges as fresh and untroubled as if it were the middle of May.

Sarcococcas come into their own in the winter, and I think because of their good evergreen foliage and complete hardiness we shall discover that 'sweet box' is being used more and more. They are plants that can easily be taken for granted in the summer, unless it is foliage and ground cover we are wanting, and I feel that hereby much winter enjoyment is missed. The flowers are small and have more tufts of stamens than normal flowers, they are white or cream and sweetly scented, and are often found adorning the top part of a neat little bush while the berries – either black or red – hang among the leaves on the lower branches.

S. humilis, with white flowers and black berries, is the most dwarf of the family, with me only about a foot high and making a rounded bush about 1½ foot wide. Obviously to make a good cover several have to be planted together, about 9 inches apart for quick cover, because these shrubs are slow growing. Among tall plants *S. ruscifolia*, which also has wide leaves (and in this case they resemble the box), white flowers, but red berries, and *S. hookeriana*, with slender willow-like leaves, pink flowers and blue-black berries, are the ones to choose. Both grow to about 3 feet and make bushes 3 to 4 feet across.

Our native daphne, *D. laureola*, could be put in the same category as the sarcoccocas as it has magnificent evergreen, glossy leaves and its scented green flowers come and go from December to April. In time it will make a bush 3 feet high by 4 feet across, and among taller trees and shrubs a planting of these shrubs is all the cover that will be needed. As the sarcococcas and the 'spurge laurel' (as the wild daphne is sometimes called) like to grow in a shady, sheltered place, they are ideal underlings.

Butcher's Broom is another dwarf green-leaved shrub suitable for underplanting shrubs. *Ruscus aculeatus* has sharply pointed oval leaves in dull dark green. To get berries it is necessary to plant male and female plants close to each other or to get the hermaphrodite form, which grows to 2½ feet and produces large scarlet berries, which lighten up darkness under trees. Butcher's Broom looks such a tough, ordinary plant that many people are inclined not to bother much about it. I know I have neglected it in the past and in consequence have lost it. It needs a shady position and should be given good soil to get it going well. *Danae racemosa* used to be called *Danae laurus**, *Ruscus racemosus* or the Alexandrian Laurel. It, too, is a plant for deep shade where it makes a compact clump of arching stems, covered with glossy leaves in bright green. It grows from 2 to 3 feet and makes a spread of about 4 feet. This plant makes excellent cut foliage for winter use.

And what about box? *Buxus sempervirens*, the common box, is not only useful for a hedge, it can also be used between shrubs in the shade or as a thick evergreen carpet in formal gardening. I have seen it filling in the space between a formal round pond and the path that encircled it, and grown like this *en masse* instead of as a hedge it looks quite a different plant. Its usual height is 3 feet and it grows about 3 feet wide.

There are several green members of the box family that can be used for ground cover, *B. microphylla* has small leaves and makes a neat, slow-growing shrub to be used when something reliable and evergreen is indicated. It grows to about 3 to 4 feet. For a dwarf cover it is best to choose box edging, *B. sempervirens suffruticosa*, which is sold by the yard. Like common box it can be kept clipped to whatever height is required.

I have seen laurels used in very big gardens to make solid blocks of green in awkward places, sometimes on a short slope between one path and another. The largest laurel is *Prunus laurocerasus caucasica*, which will reach 15 feet in time, so it needs a wide scene, but nothing could be more beautiful than its large shining green leaves. *P.* Otto Luyken is a much smaller shrub, with small pointed leaves in deep green, lined with pale green. It makes a broad spreading bush 3½ by 7 feet. The Portugal laurel, *P. lusitanica*, makes a dense and broad bush, which can be trimmed if too high. It too will grow to 15 feet and makes a bush 15 feet wide. When trimming these laurels secateurs and not shears should be used.

The less rampant bamboos will fill in spaces and discourage all weeds. The best for ground cover is the stocky little *Arundinaria pumila**, which makes foot high clumps of dark green evergreen foliage. Where something taller can be used there is *A. nitida**, a very graceful bamboo about 5 feet tall, which has slender pointed foliage in dark green on thin blue-black canes. *A. murielae** is a little taller. It has yellow stems and bright green foliage in arching plumes. Although bamboos are usually planted by water they will grow quite well in ordinary soil that is not too dry. Their graceful fluttering leaves are a joy at all times; they will grow in the shade of tall trees and are happiest in a fairly sheltered position.

~ 18 ~
Ground Cover for Banks

A bank can often be a problem in a garden. While a gentle slope covered with grass can be mowed very easily, a steep bank is awkward to cut and it is usually easier to find a way of covering it with plants that will keep tidy without too much attention.

For a sunny bank there is nothing better than thymes, and a well-clothed bank of various forms of *Thymus serpyllum* is neat, colourful and aromatic. The foliage varies in colour so that the bank is interesting even when the plants are not in flower.

Sometimes a little irregularity is preferred in the planting and then some of the bushy types of thyme can be introduced. *T. nitidus* is a small shrubby species with blue-grey leaves and soft lavender flowers. It is very aromatic and makes irregular hummocks about 1 to 1½ foot high and 3 feet across. It gives a solid effect and so does *T. vulgaris aureus*, a golden-leaved version of our common thyme. The two forms of *T. × citriodorus, T. × c. aureus* and *T. × c.* Silver Queen are a little more flimsy, making loose bushes about 9 inches high. *T. × c.* Nyewoods is a good form of golden variegation with a green central stripe down each pale yellow leaf.

Also rather shaggy but good for a large sunny bank, some of the mints and marjorams make solid rugs of foliage. Common marjoram, *Origanum vulgare*, has good dark foliage and attractive lavender flowers on 12-inch stalks. There is a compact form, *O. v. compactum*, which is neater and particularly good for ground cover. The golden-leaved form of marjoram, *O. v. aureum*, makes a solid mat of small golden foliage. It has the usual soft lavender flowers on 9-inch stalks.

A crumbling bank can be saved by *Sedum spurium*, and such a place is the only spot in a respectable garden where I would suggest introducing this sedum. The common form, with its long tough stems, fleshy leaves and flat flower heads of bright pink, is quite pretty, but it is an intruder of the worst type and every scrap will grow. But it is strong and determined enough to support tottering masonry and crumbling paths, and would certainly make a good job of a bank. In the winter there is not much to see but stems, but all through the spring, summer and autumn it is colourful and neat, and the only attention it needs is to remove the dead flowerheads if there is time. There are two named varieties with particularly bright flowers. *S. s.* Erdblut has flowers that are dark red and foliage with a tinge of bronze, and *S. s.* Schorbusser Blut, with rose red flowers on trailing stems.

Also useful on a sunny bank but only when it cannot spread elsewhere, one can use the snowy *Cerastium tomentosum*, sometimes called Snow on the Mountain or Snow in Summer.

Heathers are excellent on exposed banks, for they are used to wind and are for the most part low-growing. On lime-free soil there is infinite scope, and if there are trees at the top of the bank a very attractive trouble-free planting can be made with Kurume azaleas and heathers of various kinds, taking care that the colours do not clash. This is not likely to happen because these azaleas usually flower before the heathers although sometimes they might accidentally coincide. And there is always the colour of the foliage to be considered as well, particularly if golden heathers are used. If possible the azaleas should have broken sunlight, and they like plenty of moisture; it helps if plenty of peat or leaf-mould is added to the soil at planting time and the shrubs have a permanent mulch of chopped bracken or similar substance to keep the roots from drying out.

On limy soil there are many varieties of *Erica carnea* that can be used, and these have the great advantage of flowering in winter. The colours range from white, in *E. c.* Springwood White, with brown-stamened white flowers, the shape of tiny urns, to *E. c. vivellii*, with dark foliage and deep crimson flowers. If taller plants are wanted to break the flatness of the carnea heathers, which are all between 5 and 10 inches high, *E. darleyensis, E. mediterranea** and *E. terminalis* (*stricta*) can be interplanted, for all will grow on lime and are from 1 to 3 feet. *E. vagans*, the Cornish heath, is good for colour in summer and early autumn.

Shady banks look neatest if the plants used to cover them are naturally rather low-growing subjects such as vincas, lamiums, and bugles. The hardy geraniums that seem to prefer growing in shade are sometimes rather tall, but they sow themselves on my shady banks so that they fit into the contours. *G. ibericum, reflexum* and *punctatum** all put themselves in the shade of trees and a hybrid between *G. endressii* and *G. striatum* is particularly useful, for it makes a large clump with massed stems of foliage and flower falling down the bank. The dwarf comfrey, *Symphytum grandiflorum*, will grow in the worst possible soil and transforms a rough bank to a pleasing sheet of dark hairy foliage and hanging flowers in cream and orange. Ferns, *Saxifraga umbrosa* and its variations and the dwarf campanulas, *C. portenschlagiana* and *C. poscharskyana*, ivies and bergenias can all be used. I have a large plant of *Fatshedera* × *lizei* tumbling down one of my shady banks. Planted about half-way up the bank it makes massive shoots of large glossy leaves, topped by typical ivy flowers, which reach the top of the bank, and below lax stems with more bright foliage fall to the bottom. Even in a bad winter it will look fairly cheerful, and in a mild one it colours delightfully.

The recognised dwarf shrub for close cover on banks, whether they are shady or in the sun, is *Hypericum calycinum*, the Rose of Sharon, which is particularly useful in dense shade and on poor soil but is invasive.

For formal ground cover on banks near stately homes I have seen effective use made of clipped laurel or clipped box. *Euonymus radicans**, either plain or variegated, is expensive to begin with but attractive and permanent; the low-growing cotoneasters are a perfect choice, and in an informal garden with acid soil one could copy the natural planting of the moors and use the wild dwarf bilberry, *Vaccinium myrtillus*.

There are several shrubs that can be used for covering banks, including *Genista delphinensis** (*G. sagittalis delphinensis*) with green-winged stems which radiate from the centre of the plant and lie flat on the ground. The closely packed spikes of yellow flowers are seldom more than 6 inches along the ground and the spread of the plant can easily be up to 3 or 4 feet.

Halimiocistus sahucii is a good low-growing shrub with dark leaves and white saucer flowers. Its height is from 9 to 15 inches and it will make a spread of 6 to 8 feet. It needs good soil and a sunny site to do well.

Unfortunately *Ceretostigma plumbaginoides* (which behaves like a shrub but is classed as a herbaceous plant) loses its leaves in the winter, but its tangle of stems under the surface of the soil are thick enough to prevent weeds. It is a lovely sight in the autumn when the kingfisher blue flowers have a background of crimson leaves. Its height is only 9 inches but it will spread indefinitely, given the opportunity.

Glaucous and silver shrubs make good contrast. *Senecio laxifolius* is tough and spreading and it likes to crouch against a bank, and so does the other senecio, *S. monroii*, with wavy-edged leaves, lined with silver. I always think the glaucous *Hebe pagei** is at its best when it can fling its 3-foot stems over a wall or down a bank. In May and June each stem will be tipped with white flowers and the effect is light and harmonious.

Steep banks leading up to a house can be a problem. Usually the soil is very poor because the banks have been formed by the cutting out of a path up to the house, and one is faced with the worst possible subsoil at an acute angle.

The easiest way to deal with such banks is to start at the bottom and establish tough, clinging plants to hold up and clothe the lower part of the bank and then work on the upper reaches.

In one garden I know the banks holding up the garden above each side of the path are comparatively short but very steep. *Cotoneaster adpressa* and a dwarf New Zealand fern, *Blechnum penna marina**, are planted at the bottom of the bank, and above, a horizontal blue-grey juniper, *Juniperus chinensis pfitzeriana*, makes a thick and attractive layer of blue-grey foliage. On the top there is a smother of heathers. *Erica carnea* Springwood White and *E. c.* Springwood Pink were planted in separate layers in the beginning, but now they have intermingled and flower all through the winter.

In another garden the problem is more difficult because the path is much longer and instead of being level it is quite steep, for the house is perched high above the village street. Indifferent trees and shrubs of the elder and hazel type are growing at the top of the banks. In this village, setting something much more irregular and informal is needed. Bugles, ivies and ferns make a good lower planting for these banks, and above *Vinca major* and *Lamium galeobdolon*, planted at the top, fling themselves down the banks, rooting on their way. Primroses, sweet violets in white and purple, claytonia and dwarf campanulas are slowly spreading and covering the banks, which are of pure clay, so that each planting operation has to be done with care – and good soil.

Other plants that could have been used are *Lithospermum purpureocaeruleum*, which if planted high on the bank will send down long stems to alight here and there and make new plants of dark green. *Tellima grandiflora, Tolmiea menziesii, Heuchera viridis* and the tiny *Mitella breweri* are all suitable subjects, evergreen, and not difficult. In good soil one could use *Tiarella cordifolia*, which increases well by overground stems if it finds itself with a leafy soil and a shady site.

~ 19 ~

Ground Cover for Damp Places

Many of the plants that grow quite reasonably in normal soil will be far more luxuriant in a damp place and will grow so thickly that they can be regarded as ground cover. Bergamot, for instance, needs a damp place to do really well, for its roots are more like stems and grow close to the surface of the soil. In a damp place they are very thick and luxuriant and make a solid mat, which is quite impenetrable. Any of the named varieties can be used, but for a really good cover there is nothing better than the type plant, *Monarda didyma*, with its fascinating crimson flowers and bracts.

Herbaceous lobelias, too, grow thickly if the ground is moist enough, and such tough varieties as *L. vedrariensis*, with its fleshy leaves and tall spikes of violet flowers, and the blue *L. syphilitica* make solid rosettes of tight growing foliage. The crimson-leaved varieties are not, of course, hardy, although they often do better if the ground is moist and their fleshy roots are a good barrier against weeds.

Another rather fleshy plant, which might also be called coarse, is the white flowered *Senecio smithii*. It makes a very thick clump of dark overlapping leaves and with very little attention could be increased to make a big planting. Its daisy flowers are also fleshy and have the same solid look.

Almost invasive and certainly efficient in covering the soil, the common musk, *Mimulus luteus*, is an attractive and lusty plant and makes a wonderful show when in full bloom. Again its only fault is that it is a very ordinary plant. It works even more quickly than Creeping Jenny because the leaves are much larger and the thick fleshy roots make a matted cover that discourages all other vegetation.

There are many other varieties of mimulus but I have never had one that ramps like our British native. They are more attractive in their reds, crimsons and pinks, but their leaves are smaller and they do not increase fast – at least not for me – and usually disappear after a year or two. If the ordinary yellow-flowered mimulus is not very exciting there is *M. guttatus*, which is heavily spotted with maroon, or the hose-in-hose form, which has one flower inside another, like the duplex primroses.

Where it does not distract from other flowers the modest *Astilbe chinensis* is a quick worker for damp places, covering the soil with its delicate ferny leaves.

There are places where the sad shade of lilac-rose (which is a kind way of describing it) can be very pretty, but it needs the right background, and that it not yellow in any shade. I like to blend my magenta-pink with soft shades of powder or slaty blue or even the glaucous, bronze-tinged leaves of *Lysimachia ephemerum*.

When the problem of association is solved great pleasure can be had from this neat spreading astilbe with its 10-inch spikes of small fleshy flowers. I cannot remember when I first acquired this plant, I feel as if it had always been in my garden. I do not think of it often, but when I need something dwarf, spreading and pretty I know where to find it, and I know the clumps will be much bigger than the last time I looked, and I could easily cover large spaces with it if I took the trouble.

I have tried several times to establish other dwarf astilbes, especially *A.* × *crispa* Perkeo, but I have never succeeded, and I know of no other small astilbe with a creeping root system.

An unusual creeping plant that likes a moist position and some shade is *Houttuynia cordata*, which has all the characteristics of a Japanese plant. It does a great deal of its work underground and in a very wide area will roam far from base, but in a controlled area it makes a very close carpet of heart-shaped leaves, which are dark and tinged with metallic shades of crimson. They become almost purple in autumn. The flowers are white and have distinctive, elongated centres that stand up about ¼ inch above the petals. In the double-flowered form the blossoms look like small white rosettes. To be really happy houttuynia likes a little shade as well as moisture.

There is nothing more showy than marsh marigolds in the early part of the year, and in a damp position they grow so luxuriantly that they make wonderful ground cover. The single form of our native plant, *Caltha palustris*, is rather too robust for any but large plantings, but the double form, *C. palustris fl. pl.**, grows in a more compact way, and though it makes a large plant after it has finished flowering it always shows a certain amount of restraint. The white form is also neat in growth, it never gets out of hand but several good clumps planted about 9 inches apart cover the ground well. It has lovely flowers of pure white and is often not recognised as a marsh marigold. All these plants are easily increased by division.

Trollius can be put into the same category. The plants get bigger in their clumps but they do not spread by underground roots. As they increase quite quickly and each clump covers at least a square foot it is not necessary to have a great number to cover ground in damp positions. There are many excellent hybrids in shades varying from the old ivory of *T.* Alabaster to the richness of *T.* Orange Globe, but I still prefer the wild plant which inhabits so many damp alpine meadows in Europe. *T. europaeus* is a delightful shade of soft, greeny-yellow, which looks beautiful in any setting. The form listed by many nurseries, *T. e. superba*, is a specially fine selected form of this Globe Flower.

In the same way *Geum rivale* Leonard's Var.* is a particularly good form of our native water avens with large rosy-salmon flowers and a long season of flowering. This geum, with nodding blooms and hairy evergreen leaves, is not a large plant but it makes a clump about a foot square, and is very easily propagated by division. I grow a form with white flowers which enjoys growing in the bottom of my ditch garden, where the soil is moist. It makes quite large clumps and sows itself in a quiet way.

The South American *Verbena corymbosa* is usually described as 'rampageous', rooting where it touches the ground, but it does not do this in dry soil. In a damp position it grows most luxuriantly, making thick vegetation about 3 feet high with scented violet-purple heads. Where it is happy there is no restraining it, but it does not grow well for everybody. I have planted it half a dozen times but have never established it, although I have given it the dampest spots in the garden from which to choose a home. It may dislike the lime in my soil, although all the other verbenas I know raise no objections.

That rampant moisture-loving grass, *Glyceria aquatica variegata**, has no such inhibitions. It is ground cover of the most robust kind, with handsome striped leaves.

There are several ferns which prefer to grow in moist soil, some of which make excellent ground cover. *Onoclea sensibilis* is a marsh-loving fern with a running root-stock, particularly good in damp soil under trees where its colonising habits can be appreciated. It has handsome, rather bold leaves about 18 inches high, and makes a clump about a foot square. The ostrich fern, matteuccia, also thrives on moisture, but does not benefit to such an extent that it runs all over the place. It has very dainty leaves, much divided and especially beautiful in early spring when they are fresh and young.

Blechnum tabulare is not as hardy as the other two, but it also needs a moist soil. In very cold districts it should be covered with bracken in winter, and is evergreen only in sheltered areas. It has graceful 2-foot leaves in dark green divided into pinnae about ½ inch wide.

One can hardly call the regal fern, *Osmunda regalis*, ground cover and yet nothing else will intrude where this majestic fern is established. It likes a very moist position, even at the edge of a pond or stream, and then will throw up its 4-foot leaves, which are beautiful from the moment they appear like crosiers and unfurl to show their glinting shades of copper-brown. Even when fully opened there is always a rich feeling of coppery-brown behind the green.

Many of the plants that do well in damp places are not orthodox ground cover, but they will grow so thickly that they discourage all weeds. Candelabra primulas in the right conditions come up like mustard and cress and make a forest of foliage, and other bog primulas such as *P. florindae* and *helodoxa* will do the same, but of course they are not evergreen.

In the same way lythrum seeds itself thickly and again is not evergreen, but the roots are woody and discourage weeds. There are several good named varieties of *L. salicaria*, Brightness, Lady Sackville, Robert and The Beacon.

The heavy stem roots of *Peltiphyllum peltatum*, the umbrella plant, grow so close together that nothing could grow through them. The pale pink flowers on stiff stems open in April before the leaves, which are about 6 inches across. A good planting of rodgersia, either the pink flowered *R. aesculifolia, R. pinnata* in rose or white, or *R. tabularis* with cream flowers, make wonderful thickets of handsome foliage and feathery flowers; massive plants of rhubarb, which does best in a damp position, will solve the ground cover problem for many square yards. My favourite is *Rheum palmatum atrosanguineum*, with crimson flowers on 6-foot spikes and crimson linings to the great leaves. *R. nobile* has shining green leaves, greenish flowers and straw-coloured bracts.

The enormous leaves of *Lysichitum americanum* will cover a square yard of soil. They are green in *L. americanum*, to go with the yellow taum flowers, smaller and more grey-green in *L. camtschatcense*, with its white flowers. Gunneras, of course, are only for a very big garden, for they can make a plant up to 20 feet across, with leaves 6 feet wide, but they cover the ground and keep out weeds.

~ 20 ~
Plants for Poor Soils

There are some plants that cannot be allowed anywhere near good soil as they would never know when to stop; even poor soil does not discourage them, so they have their uses when there are very difficult places that have to be clothed.

Cerastium tomentosum should, I think, be given pride of place. Out of interest I looked through a dozen nursery catalogues and not one of them lists it, not even the nursery that offers its customers that other menace, *Veronica filiformis*. And that shows how persistent Snow in Summer can be. For years I have been advising gardeners who want to plant it on rock gardens never to let it nearer to civilisation than the top of a wall that has no flower bed near it.

But for our very bad soil and our difficult corners where nothing else will grow *Cerastium tomentosum* will take over. It is a really attractive plant, with its white woolly leaves and hundreds of delicate white flowers. It shows up well against red brick, and if the background is rather neutral one could sow the red-leaved spinach, *Atriplex hortensis*, which will also tolerate poor conditions and would show up well behind cerastium. I would never recommend this plant if it can escape into more civilised parts of the garden, for it is quite without conscience and will steam roller anything in its path.

Hieracium aurantiacum spreads, but it does it in a more honest way. Cerastium infiltrates with slender but determined white roots, which will penetrate paving and work round stones and under walls, but hieracium is always above-board, sending out long leafy runners which form rosettes and root as they go. Its country name is Fox and Cubs, or Grim the Cobbler, because of the black hairs under the flowers, and it is a bright, tough customer with orange flowers and coarse hairy leaves. It will grow in sun or shade and no soil is too bad for it. Its rosettes grow flat on the ground and it is quite capable of holding up a steep bank with a strong leafy mat. Some people grow a form that has flowers more vermilion than orange, but it remains a firebrand only acceptable in dull dark places where its strident tones are blurred by shade.

Symphytum glandiflorum will grow in very poor soil too, and seems to delight in the worse type of clay, but though it will grow well in sun it is even more industrious in shade. It too has dark, coarse hairy leaves and increases by long, tough stems. It is not such a neat worker as hieracium. Although it appears to be making a dense carpet not all the new rosettes are anchored by roots. This does not affect its value as ground cover, but if one wants to dig up a plant it is sometimes difficult to find nicely rooted specimens suitable for transplanting.

The taller symphytums will also grow in poor soil and make good ground cover in places where 3-foot plants are suitable. The wild comfrey that grows in our hedgerows suppresses all weeds and the cultivated symphytums do just as well, particularly in woodland gardens where there is plenty of room. And they will grow in the poorest soil. *S. tauricum* has white flowers and though it does not spread it seeds itself liberally, rather too liberally in some parts of the garden, but not when it is needed to cover poor ground. *S. peregrinum* has sky-blue flowers, opening from pink buds, and is not so prolific with its seedlings. Nor is the deep blue *S. caucasicum*, which is a more restrained plant, growing only to 2 feet and having narrow blue-grey leaves. But it too will grow anywhere and is particularly useful for growing in poor soil under trees.

That great hairy borage, *Trachystemon orientalis*, will put up its massive leaves and produce its small blue flowers in the poor soil under trees. It is a heavy, coarse plant but is useful when something really big and smothering can be used.

In my garden *Brunnera macrophylla* (which most of us still think of as *Anchusa myosotidiflora**) seems to choose the worst bits of soil and flourishes everywhere. In its early stages it is a neat and attractive plant, with small, neat packed leaves, but when it gets coarse and leafy it is pleasant to relegate it to the barren wastes under trees.

There too will grow the hart's tongue fern, *Phyllitis scolopendrium*, which seems to get on with very little soil and from the smallest space will produce a huge rosette of rich green strap-like fronds, waved at the edges and sometimes double fanged.

It always seems wasteful to plant *Carex pendula* in good soil because it does just as well in the worst places in the garden. This coarse, good-tempered grass makes quite pleasant furnishing for places which would otherwise be ugly and bare, and is very graceful when its arching stems are in flower. I know one garden where it has planted itself with its back to the end of a wall that screens the kitchen quarters, and it makes a pleasant screen throughout the year. Another place where I see it regularly is in a neglected vicarage garden. The house is divided and the approach to one flat is humanised by great clumps of this grass in what would otherwise be a most depressing and desolate corner.

Our wild iris, *I. foetidissima*, will grow in the most dreadful soil and it too has the pleasant habit of seeding itself in dusty corners and under trees. In my village there is an enormous clump against the entrance to a farmyard. The iris is growing against a wall at the edge of the asphalt footpath and cannot have any soil at all, and yet the wide dark green leaves are always glossy with health and in the autumn make a setting for many open pods of orange seeds.

The variegated form of the Gladwin or stinking iris is not fussy about soil either. Someone must have put a scrap in a most unattractive bed by a little brick house I know. The soil is yellow clay and nothing else grows in it, but the iris has increased until now it fills the whole bed and looks beautiful against the harsh red brick. In another garden where the soil is most unpromising it does so well that the owners have to throw it away in large quantities. I try to be there when this painful operation takes place and offer a better home than the compost heap.

Plants that become a nuisance in a normal flower bed are often quite welcome in the difficult places where nothing else will grow. I once grew *Salvia verticillata* from seed and put a few plants in a bed with good herbaceous plants and very soon the salvia was everywhere, filling all the space with its long prostrate stems covered with hairy grey leaves and furnished with small blue flowers. When I moved it, and a white flowered form, to a rough bank I felt far more affection for the plant.

In the same way I am very fond of *Lamium maculatum* when it makes a mat of neat foliage among the roots of trees, but I resent it smothering my special plants in normal flower beds. This evergreen plant, with its silvered leaves and magenta-pink flowers, will thrive in the poorest soil and is quite attractive under trees or on steep banks. Sometimes a carpeting plant is needed to cover the ground under hedges and this lamium is ideal for the job.

L. orvala is not a carpeter but it makes comfortably spreading plants about 2 feet high which serve as dense weed smother. It will take over the worst possible places under trees or on bare banks and completely furnish them. This is a completely herbaceous plant, dying down in the winter and reappearing in spring. It seeds itself well. The species *L. orvala* has rosy-lilac flowers and hairy soft green nettle leaves, tinged with red, and there is a variety of it, *L. o. album*, which has white flowers and soft green leaves, without a trace of red. Though not very exciting this lamium has a pleasant old-fashioned air which reminds one of old gardens and country cottages.

Motherwort, *Leonurus cardiaca*, is not such a colourful plant, but it has very pretty velvety green leaves which make neat rosettes. It appears in the most unlikely places and soon covers the soil, however poor it happens to be. This plant does not make a thicket as does *Lamium orvala*, but the ground cover is quite effective and the 2-foot flower spikes with their whorls of furry pinkish-purple flowers stand up straight and tall and make attractive winter skeletons. It is faintly aromatic and so is balm, *Melissa officinalis*, which also makes a close carpet of crinkled dark green leaves. Its flowers are white and by no means striking, but it is a pleasant old-fashioned herb which will grow anywhere and has no vice except a mild tendency to seed.

The burnets are pleasant plants which will grow in the poorest soil. We used to know them as poterium, but now sanguisorba is the name under which they are listed. They all have bottle-brush flower heads, and neat ferny leaves. The most common is *S. obtusa* with mauve-pink flowers, and its white form *S. o. alba*. It is a runner and I had to banish it from a flower bed because it became such a nuisance. But in places which need such exuberance it is a good plant. The tall *S. canadensis* does not run and its strong straight stems rise to 6 feet against the modest 2½ feet of *S. obtusa*. *S. officinalis* is a native plant that flowers from June to September and has many small heads of crimson flowers. I grow a bronze form of salad burnet, *S. minor* (*Poterium sanguisorba*), which has small greeny bronze heads and particularly pretty leaves. It grows about a foot high and smells of cucumber when crushed. No soil is too bad for it; I grow it in a stony bed of pure clay and it does quite well.

Nothing will stop the strong thrusting roots of our native crane's bill. It has good leaves, which colour in autumn, and an endless succession of large magenta flowers, which give it its name of *Geranium sanguineum*, the bloody crane's bill, a name it deserves when it burrows under its betters and disintegrates walls. But it will hold together a crumbling bank and produces flowers all through the season.

G. endressii will grow anywhere and is a more easily managed plant because it does most of its work on top of the soil, making heavy mats of stems, and flowers almost endlessly.

The growing habit of G. *macrorrhizum* is a cross between the other two. It is more dwarf and colours better if grown in poor soil.

The rather rampant purple gromwell, *Lithospermum purpureo-caeruleum*, will grow where nothing else will survive. It is an excellent plant for dry, chalky places, limestone, scrub and stony, hungry soil. Its long adventuring stems are clothed with narrow, dark green leaves, and wherever they come to rest, after flinging themselves down banks and over ledges, they root, and the same thing starts all over again. The flowers of very dark blue, opening from reddish buds, are lovely from May to July.

Plant-Name Changes

In her writings Margery Fish naturally used the plant names that were familiar to her and which were considered acceptable at the time. But times have changed, and while many of the names she used are still current, and many that are not are nevertheless recognisable, some have changed completely.

So to help contemporary gardeners understand exactly which plants Mrs Fish is discussing, we have given the current accepted name alongside the name Mrs Fish used where we feel this is helpful. This has caused problems.

In some cases Mrs Fish gives two different names for the same plant, yet modern thinking may apply these two names to two different entities. She may also give two different names for what she asserts are two different plants yet modern thinking assures us that the two plants are the same. In some cases she indicates that one name has been superseded by another while it may now be clear that the first name, or another name altogether, is actually correct. Occasionally, Mrs Fish uses a name that has never been valid; sometimes it's clear that this is simply a misspelling, sometimes the origin of the mistake is less obvious; a little detective work has usually revealed her intent.

So while acknowledging that an entirely accurate explanation of these nomenclatural niceties would be impossible without many cumbersome footnotes, we hope that our additions will prove helpful. In identifying the correct names we sought advice and clarification from *The PlantFinder*, a range of modern encyclopedias and monographs together with expert individuals. But Mrs Fish grew such an extraordinary range of plants, some obscure even by today's standards and some now completely lost, that a few minor problems remain unresolved.

In general we have changed Mrs Fish's original text as little as possible but the accepted manner in which names are styled in type has also changed over the years. So in some cases we have simply modified the expression of an otherwise correct name in order to avoid unnecessary additions.

The science of plant nomenclature perhaps should be, but is certainly not, a precise one; however, we feel sure that by making these additions we add to an appreciation of Mrs Fish's writing and of the plants she grew.

Graham Rice

Plant name in the text	Correct current name
Abies nobilis glauca prostrata	*Abies procera* 'Glauca Prostrata'
Abies procera glauca prostrata	*Abies procera* 'Glauca Prostrata'
Acaena adscendens	*Acaena saccaticupula* 'Blue Haze'
Acaena glauca	*Acaena caesiglauca*
Acaena microphylla inermis	*Acaena inermis*
Acaena novae-zealandiae	*Acaena novae-zelandiae*
Acaena sanguisorbae	*Acaena anserinifola*
Acanthus latifolius	*Acanthus mollis* Latifolius Group
Achillea clavenae	*Achillea clavennae*
Achillea wilczeckiana	*Achillea* Wilczekii
Actaea spicata alba	*Actaea pachypoda*
Ageratum mexicanum	*Ageratum houstonianum*
Ajuga reptans multicolor	*Ajuga reptans* 'Multicolor'
Ajuga reptans Rainbow	*Ajuga reptans* 'Multicolor'
Alopecursus pratensis foliis variegatis	*Alopecurus pratensis* 'Aureovariegatus'
Alyssum maritimum	*Lobularia maritima*
Amsonia salicifolia	*Amsonia tabernaemontana var. salicifolia*
Anchusa myosotidiflora	*Brunnera macrophylla*
Anemone St Brigid	*Anemone coronaria* Saint Brigid Group
Antennaria rubra	*Antennaria dioica* 'Rubra'
Antennaria tomentosa	*Antennaria dioica* var. *hyperborea*
Anthemis cupaniana	*Anthemis punctata* subsp. *cupaniana*
Anthemis nobilis	*Chamaemelum nobile*
Anthemis nobilis fl. pl.	*Chamaemelum nobile* 'Flore Pleno'
Arabis albida	*Arabis alpina* subsp. *caucasica*
Armeria caespitosa Bevan's Var.	*Armeria juniperifolia* 'Bevan's Variety'
Armeria Corsica	*Armeria maritima* 'Corsica'
Armeria laucheana	*Armeria maritima* 'Laucheana'
Armeria plantaginea	*Armeria alliacea*
Arrhenatherum elatius bulbosum variegatum	*Arrhenatherum elatius* subsp. *bulbosum* 'Variegatum'
Artemisia Lambrook Silver	*Artemisia absinthium* 'Lambrook Silver'
Artemisia pedemontana	*Artemisia caucasica*
Artemisia schmidtii	*Artemisia schmidtiana*
Arum corsicum	*Arum pictum*
Arum italicum marmoratum	*Arum italicum* subsp. *italicum* 'Marmoratum'
Aruncus sylvester	*Aruncus dioicus*

Arundinaria murielae	*Fargesia murieliae*
Arundinaria nitida	*Fargesia nitida*
Arundinaria pumila	*Pleioblastus humilis* var. *pumilis*
Asperula odorata	*Gallium odoratum*
Aster Snow Cushion	*Aster novi-belgii* 'Schneekissen'
Astrantia helleborifolia	*Astrantia maxima*
Berberis thunbergii atropurpurea	*Berberis thunbergii* f. *atropurpurea*
Berberis thunbergii atropurpurea nana	*Berberis thunbergii* 'Atropurpurea Nana'
Bergenia Ballawley Hybrid	*Bergenia* 'Ballawley'
Bergenia cordifolia Miss Jekyll's Form	*Bergenia cordifolia* 'Purpurea'
Bergenia cordifolia purpurea	*Bergenia cordifolia* 'Purpurea'
Bergenia delavayi	*Bergenia purpurascens* var. *delavayi*
Blechnum penna marina	*Blechnum penna-marina*
Buxus suffruiticosa	*Buxus sempervirens* 'Suffruticosa'
Calluna vulgaris Co. Wicklow	*Calluna vulgaris* 'County Wicklow'
Calluna serlei aurea	*Calluna vulgaris* 'Serlei Aurea'
Caltha palustris fl. pl.	*Caltha palustris* 'Flore Pleno'
Campanula acaulis	*Campanula glomerata* var. *acaulis*
Campanula muralis	*Campanula portenschlagiana*
Cardamine asarifolia	*Pachyphragma macrophyllum*
Cardamine aurea	*Barbarea vulgaris* 'Variegata'
Cardamine latifolia	*Cardamine raphinifolia*
Centaurea gymnocarpa	*Centaurea cineraria*
Chamaecyparis lawsoniana fletcheri	*Chamaecyparis lawsoniana* 'Fletcheri'
Chrysanthemum haradjanii	*Tanacetum haradjanii*
C. parthenium White Bonnet	*Tanacetum parthenium* 'White Bonnet'
Cistus corbariensis	*Cistus* x *hybridus*
Cistus loretii	*Cistus* x *dansereaui*
Cistus x *lusitanicus decumbens*	*Cistus* x *dansereaui* 'Decumbens'
Cistus Warley Rose	*Cistus* x *crispatus* 'Warley Rose'
Clematis davidiana	*Clematis tubulosa*
Clematis jouiniana	*Clematis* x *jouiana*
Clematis praecox	*Clematis* x *jouiana* 'Praecox'
Coronilla glauca	*Coronilla valentina* subsp. *glauca*
Cotinus coggygria purpureus	*Cotinus coggygria* Purpureus Group
Cotoneaster Autumn Fire	*Cotoneaster salicifolius* 'Herbstfeuer'
Cotoneaster congesta procumbens	*Cotoneaster congestus* 'Nanus'
Cotoneaster hybrida pendula	*Cotoneaster* 'Hybridus Pendulus'
Cotoneaster integerrima Arnold Forster	*Cotoneaster prostratus* 'Arnold Forster'

Cotoneaster Sabrina	*Cotoneaster splendens*
Cotula pyrethrifolia	*Leptinella pyrethrifolia*
Cotula squalida	*Leptinella squalida*
Daboëcia alba	*Daboëcia cantabrica* f. *alba*
Daboëcia atropurpurea	*Daboëcia cantabrica* 'Atropurpurea'
Daboëcia bicolor	*Daboëcia cantabrica* 'Bicolor'
Danae laurus	*Danae racemosa*
Daphne Somerset	*Daphne* x *burkwoodii* 'Somerset'
Dianthus Inglescombe	*Dianthus* 'Inglestone'
Dianthus Musgrave's White	*Dianthus* 'Musgrave's Pink'
Dimorphotheca barberiae	*Osteospermum jucundum*
Dimorphotheca ecklonis	*Osteospermum ecklonis*
Doronicum Harpur Crewe	*Doronicum* x *excelsum* 'Harpur Crewe'
Dorycnium hirsutum	*Lotus hirsutum*
Dracocephalum prattii	*Nepeta prattii*
Elymus glaucus	*Elymus hispidus*
Epimedium pinnatum colchicum	*Epimedium pinnatum* subsp. *colchicum*
Erica mediterranea	*Erica erigena*
Erigeron mucronatus	*Erigeron karvinskianus*
Euonymus radicans	*Euonymus fortunei* var. *radicans*
Euonymus coloratus	*Euonymus fortunei* 'Coloratus'
Euonymus kewensis	*Euonymus fortunei* 'Kewensis'
Euonymus minimus	*Euonymus fortunei* 'Minimus'
Euonymus Silver Queen	*Euonymus fortunei* 'Silver Queen'
Euphorbia robbiae	*Euphorbia amygdaloides* var. *robbiae*
Euphorbia sibthorpii	*E. characias* subsp. *wulfenii* var. *sibthorpii*
Euphorbia wulfenii	*Euphorbia characias* subsp. *wulfenii*
Fragaria indica	*Duchesnea indica*
Galax aphylla	*Galax urceolata*
Gaultheria minuta	*Gaultheria nummularioides* var. *elliptica*
Gaultheria nummularifolia	*Gaultheria nummularioides*
Genista delphinensis	*Genista sagittalis* subsp. *delphinensis*
Geranium atlanticum	*Geranium malviflorum*
Geranium endressii Wargrave	*Geranium* x *oxonianum* 'Wargrave Pink'
Geranium grevilleanum	*Geranium lambertii*
Geranium ibericum	*Geranium* x *magnificum*
Geranium ibericum platypetalum	*Geranium* x *magnificum*
Geranium macrorrhizum album	*Geranium macrorrhizum* 'Album'
Geranium punctatum	*Geranium* x *monacense* 'Muldoon'

Geranium sanguineum lancastriense	*Geranium sanguineum* var. *striatum*
Geranium traversii Russell Prichard	*G.* x *riversleaianum* 'Russell Prichard'
Geranium wallichianum Buxton's Blue	*Geranium wallichianum* 'Buxton's Variety'
Geum x *borisii*	*Geum* 'Borisii'
Geum rivale Leonard's Var.	*Geum rivale* 'Leonard's Variety'
Glyceria aquatica variegata	*Glyceria maxima* var. *variegata*
Hebe catarractae	*Parahebe catarractae*
Hebe pagei	*Hebe pinguifolia* 'Pagei'
Hedera canariensis variegata	*Hedera canariensis* 'Gloire de Marengo'
Hedera chrysocarpa	*Hedera helix* f. *poetarum*
Hedera colchica dentata variegata	*Hedera colchica* 'Dentata Variegata'
Hedera congesta	*Hedera helix* 'Congesta'
Hedera coriacea purpurea	*Hedera colchica*
Hedera grandifolia	*Hedera canariensis*
Hedera helix angularis aurea	*Hedera helix* 'Angularis Aurea'
Hedera helix caenwoodiana	*Hedera helix* 'Pedata'
Hedera helix Chicago aurea	*Hedera helix* 'Buttercup'
Hedera helix conglomerata	*Hedera helix* 'Conglomerata'
Hedera helix cristata	*Hedera helix* 'Parsley Crested'
Hedera helix Curly Locks	*Hedera helix* 'Manda's Crested'
Hedera helix deltoidea	*Hedera hibernica* 'Deltoidea'
Hedera helix elegantissima	*Hedera helix* 'Tricolor'
Hedera helix Emerald Green	*Hedera helix* f. *poetarum*
Hedera helix feastii	*Hedera helix* 'Königer'
Hedera helix Jubilee Gold Heart	*Hedera helix* 'Oro di Bogliasco'
Hedera helix lucida	*Hedera helix* f. *poetarum*
Hedera helix Lutzii	*Hedera helix* 'Luzii'
Hedera helix maculata	*Hedera helix* 'Minor Marmorata'
Hedera helix marginata rubra	*Hedera helix* 'Tricolor'
Hedera helix marginata tricolor	*Hedera helix* 'Tricolor'
Hedera helix marmorata	*Hedera helix* 'Luzii'
Hedera helix minima	*Hedera helix* 'Donerailensis'
Hedera helix pedata Grey Arrow	*Hedera helix* 'Pedata'
Hedera helix pedata Heron	*Hedera helix* 'Heron'
Hedera helix sagittaefolia	*Hedera helix* 'Sagittifolia'
Hedera helix Silver Queen	*Hedera helix* 'Tricolor'
Hedera Nielson	*Hedera helix* 'Neilson'
Hedera poetica	*Hedera helix* f. *poetarum*
Hedera purpurea	*Hedera helix* 'Atropurpurea'

Helleborus abchasicus	Helleborus orientalis subsp. *abchasicus*
Helleborus Apotheker Bogren	Helleborus x hybridus 'Apotheker Bogren'
Helleborus Apple Blossom	Helleborus x hybridus 'Apple Blossom'
Helleborus atrorubens 'Early Purple'	Helleborus orientalis subsp. *abchasicus*
Helleborus Aurora	Helleborus x hybridus 'Aurora'
Helleborus corsicus	Helleborus argutifolius
Helleborus intermedius	Helleborus torquatus
Helleborus kochii	Helleborus orientalis
Helleborus olympicus	Helleborus orientalis
Helleborus Potter's Wheel	Helleborus niger 'Potters Wheel'
Helxine soleirolii	Soleirolia soleirolii
Hemerocallis fulva fl. pl.	Hemerocallis fulva 'Flore Pleno'
Heuchera tiarelloides	Heucherella tiarelloides
Hieracium aurantiacum	Pilosella aurantiaca
Hieracium pilosella	Pilosella officinarum
Holcus lanatus variegatus	Holcus mollis 'Albovariegatus'
Hosta albomarginata	Hosta 'Paxton's Original'
Hosta coerulea	Hosta ventricosa
Hosta fortunei albopicta	Hosta fortunei var. *albopicta*
Hosta fortunei robusta	Hosta sieboldiana var. *elegans*
Hosta glauca	Hosta sieboldiana var. *elegans*
Hosta sieboldiana robusta	Hosta sieboldiana var. *elegans*
Hosta Thomas Hogg	Hosta undulata var. *albomarginata*
Hydrangea petiolaris	Hydrangea anomala subsp. *petiolaris*
Hypericum elatum Elstead Var.	Hypericum x inodorum 'Elstead'
Hypericum x moserianum tricolor	Hypericum x moserianum 'Tricolor'
Hypericum reptans	Hypericum olympicum var. *minus*
Iberis sempervirens garrexiana	Iberis sempervirens
Iberis sempervirens Little Gem	Iberis sempervirens 'Weisser Zwerg'
Iberis sempervirens Snowflake	Iberis sempervirens 'Schneeflocke'
Indigofera floribunda	Indigofera heterantha
Indigofera gerardiana	Indigofera heterantha
Juniperus Blue Danube	Juniperus sabina 'Blaue Donau'
Juniperus chinensis expansa variegate	Juniperus chinensis 'Expansa Variegata'
Juniperus pfitzeriana	Juniperus x pfitzeriana
Juniperus pfitzeriana aurea	Juniperus x pfitzeriana 'Pfitzeriana Aurea'
Juniperus pfitzeriana compacta	J. x pfitzeriana 'Pfitzeriana Compacta'
Juniperus pfitzeriana glauca	Juniperus x pfitzeriana 'Pfitzeriana Glauca'
Juniperus saxatilis	Juniperus communis var. *saxatilis*

Juniperus conferta	Juniperus rigidus subsp. conferta
Juniperus Grey Owl	Juniperus virginiana 'Grey Owl'
Juniperus Hicksii	Juniperus sabina 'Hicksii'
Juniperus horizontalis douglasii	Juniperus horizontalis 'Douglasii'
Juniperus horizontalis plumosa	Juniperus horizontalis 'Plumosa'
Juniperus litoralis	Juniperus conferta
Juniperus sabina tamariscifolia	Juniperus sabina 'Tamariscifolia'
Lamium galeobdolon variegatum	Lamium galeobdolon subsp. montanum 'Florentinum'
Lavandula Folgate Purple	Lavandula angustifolia 'Folgate'
Lavandula Gwendolen Anley	Lavandula 'Gwendolyn Anley'
Lavandula Hidcote Purple	Lavandula angustifolia 'Hidcote'
Lavandula Twickle Purple	Lavandula angustifolia 'Twickel Purple'
Leiophyllum prostratum	Leiophyllum buxifolium var. prostratum
Linaria aequitriloba	Cymbalaria aequitriloba
Lippia canascens	Phyla canescens
Lippia repens	Phyla nodiflora
Liriope graminifolia	Liriope muscari
Lithosprmum diffusum	Lithodora diffusa
Lithospermum album	Lithodora diffusa 'Album'
Lithospermum Grace Ward	Lithodora diffusa 'Grace Ward'
Lithospermum Heavenly Blue	Lithodora diffusa 'Heavenly Blue'
Lithospermum prostratum	Lithodora diffusa 'Grace Ward'
Lithospermum purpureo-caeruleum	Buglossoides purpureocaerulea
Lobelia syphilitica	Lobelia siphilitica
Lobelia vedrariensis	Lobelia x gerardii 'Vedrariensis'
Lonicera japonica aureo-reticulata	Lonicera japonica 'Aureoreticulata'
Lonicera japonica halliana	Lonicera japonica 'Halliana'
Lychnis coronaria Abbotswood Rose	Lychnis x walkeri 'Abbotswood Rose'
Lysichitum americanum	Lysichiton americanus
Lysichitum camtschtcense	Lysichiton camtschatcensis
Lysimachia japonica minuta	Lysimachia japonica var. minutissima
Lysimachia verticillata	Lysimachia verticillaris
Lythrum Brightness	Lythrum salicaria 'Brightness'
Lythrum Lady Sackville	Lythrum salicaria 'Lady Sackville'
Lythrum Robert	Lythrum salicaria 'Robert'
Lythrum The Beacon	Lythrum salicaria 'The Beacon'
Mahonia aquifolium atropurpurea	Mahonia aquifolium 'Atropurpurea'
Mahonia aquifolium undulata	Mahonia x wagneri 'Undulata'

Mentha x gentilis aurea	Mentha x gracilis 'Variegata'
Mentha rotundifolia variegata	Mentha suaveolens 'Variegata'
Menziesia polifolia	Daböecia cantabrica 'Polifolia'
Milium effusum aureum	Milium effusum 'Aureum'
Mulgedium bourgaei	Lactuca bourgaei
Nemophila menziesii alba	Nemophila menziesii var. atomaria
Nepeta Six Hills Variety	Nepeta 'Six Hills Giant'
Oenothera missouriensis	Oenothera macrocarpa
Oenothera taraxicifolia	Oenothera acaulis
Ophiopogon spicatus	Liriope muscari
Othonnopsis cheirifolia	Othonna cheirifolia
Oxalis floribunda	Oxalis articulata
Oxalis rosea	Oxalis racemosa
Parthenocissus inconstans	Parthenocissus tricuspidata
Peltiphyllum peltatum	Darmera peltata
Pernettya Bell's Seedling	Gaultheria mucronata 'Bell's Seedling'
Pernettya mucronata alba	Gaultheria mucronata 'Alba'
Pernettya mucronata Donard Pink	Gaultheria mucronata 'Donard Pink'
Pernettya mucronata Donard White	Gaultheria mucronata 'Donard White'
Pernettya mucronata lilacina	Gaultheria mucronata 'Lilacina'
Pernettya mucronata rosea coccinea	Gaultheria mucronata 'Rosea Coccinea'
Pernettya mucronata rubra lilacina	Gaultheria mucronata 'Rubra Lilacina'
Phalaris arundinacea picta	Phalaris arundinacea 'Picta'
Phlomis russelliana	Phlomis russeliana
Phlomis samia	Phlomis russeliana
Phlomis viscosa	Phlomis russeliana
Phlox douglasii Boothman's Var.	Phlox douglasii 'Boothman's Variety'
Phlox douglasii rosea	Phlox douglasii 'Rosea'
Phlox Sprite	Phlox douglasii 'Sprite'
Phlox subulata G. F. Wilson	Phlox subulata 'Lilacina'
Phlox subulata Temiscaming	Phlox subulata 'Temiskaming'
Phyllitis scolopendrium	Asplenium scolopendrium
Physalis franchetii	Physalis alkekengii var. franchetii
Picea abies procumbens	Picea abies 'Procumbens'
Picea pungens glauco-procumbens	Picea pungens 'Glauca Procumbens'
Polygonatum officinale	Polygonatum odoratum
Polygonum affine	Persicaria affinis
Polygonum affine Darjeeling Red	Persicaria affinis 'Darjeeling Red'
Polygonum baldschuanicum	Fallopia baldschuanica

Polygonum campanulatum	Persicaria campanulata
Polygonum capitatum	Persicaria capitata
Polygonum cuspidatum	Fallopia japonica
Polygonum cuspidatum compactum	Fallopia japonica var. compacta
Polygonum emodii	Persicaria emodii
Polygonum reynoutria	Fallopia japonica
Polygonum vacciniifolium	Persicaria vaccinifolia
Potentilla argyrophylla	Potentilla atrosanguinea var. argyrophylla
Potentilla fruticosa arbuscula	Potentilla fruticosa 'Elizabeth'
Potentilla Miss Willmott	Potentilla nepalensis 'Miss Willmott'
Potentilla Roxana	Potentilla nepalensis 'Roxana'
Poterium sanguisorba	Sanguisorba minor
Pratia treadwellii	Pratia angulata 'Treadwellii'
Primula Garryarde Guinevere	Primula 'Guinevere'
Primula helodoxa	Primula prolifera
Prunella incisa rubra	Prunella vulgaris var. rubra
Prunella Loveliness	Prunella grandiflora 'Loveliness'
Prunella webbiana	Prunella grandiflora
Prunus laurocerasus caucasica	Prunus laurocerasus 'Caucasica'
Prunus Otto Luyken	Prunus laurocerasus 'Otto Luyken'
Pterecephalus parnassii	Pterecephalus perennis
Raoulia australis	Raoulia hookeri
Raoulia lutescens	Raoulia australis Lutescens Group
Rhazya orientalis	Amsonia orientalis
Rheum palmatum atrosanguineum	Rheum palmatum 'Atrosanguineum'
Rhododendron forrestii repens	Rhododendron forrestii Repens Group
Rhododendron keleticum	Rhododendron calostrotum subsp. keleticum
Rhododendron lapponicum complexum	Rhododendron complexum
Rhododendron radicans	Rhododendron calostrotum subsp. keleticum Radicans Group
Rhus canadensis	Rhus aromatica
Rhus cotinus folius purpureis	Cotinus coggygria 'Foliis Purpureis'
Rodgersia tabularis	Astilboides tabularis
Rosa Dr van Fleet	Rosa 'Doctor W. van Fleet'
Rosa x macrantha	Rosa 'Macrantha'
Rosa x macrantha Daisy Hill	Rosa 'Daisy Hill'
Rosa x macrantha Raubritter	Rosa 'Raubritter'

Rosa paulii	Rosa 'Paulii'
Rosa rugosa Frau Dagmar Hastrup	Rosa 'Frau Dagmar Hastrup'
Rosa rugosa Max Graf	Rosa x jacksonii 'Max Graf'
Rosa rugosa repens alba	Rosa 'Paulii'
Rosa rugosa Schneelicht	Rosa 'Schneelicht'
Rosa Sander's White	Rosa 'Sander's White Rambler'
Rosa wichuraiana	Rosa wichurana
Rosmarinus lavandulaceus	Rosmarinus officinalius Prostratus Group
Rosmarinus officinalis prostratus	Rosmarinus officinalius Prostratus Group
Rubus fockeanus	Rubus pentalobus
Rubus ulmifolius bellidiflorus	Rubus ulmifolius 'Bellidiflorus'
Ruscus racemosus	Danae racemosa
Sagina glabra	Sagina subulata var. glabrata
Sagina glabra aurea	Sagina subulata var. glabrata 'Aurea'
Sagina subulata	Sagina subulata var. glabrata
Sagina subulata aurea	Sagina subulata var. glabrata 'Aurea'
Salvia officinalis purpurascens	Salvia officinalis 'Purpurascens'
Salvia officinalis tricolor	Salvia officinalis 'Tricolor'
Salvia sclarea turkestanica	Salvia sclarea var. sclarea
Sanguisobora obtusa alba	Sanguisobora albiflora
Santolina chamaecyparissus nana	Santolina chamaecyparissus var. nana
Santolina incana	Santolina chamaecyparissus
Santolina Lemon Queen	Santolina chamaecyparissus 'Lemon Queen'
Santolina neapolitana	Santolina pinnata subsp. neapolitana
Santolina neapolitana sulphurea	Santolina pinnata subsp. neapolitana 'Sulphurea'
Santolina serratifolia	Santolina rosmarinifolia subsp. canescens
Santolina virens	Santolina rosmarinifolia subsp. rosmarinifolia
Santolina viridis	Santolina rosmarinifolia subsp. rosmarinifolia
Saxifraga geum	Saxifraga x geum
Saxifraga hynoides gemmifera	Saxifraga hynoides
Saxifraga kingil	Saxifraga 'Egemmulosa'
Saxifraga Mrs Piper	Saxifraga 'Mrs E. Piper'

Saxifraga sarmentosa	Saxifraga stolonifera
Saxifraga Sir D. Haig	Saxifraga 'Sir Douglas Haig'
Saxifraga umbrosa geum	Saxifraga x geum
Scabiosa pterocephalus	Pterocephalus perennis
Scabiosa rumelica	Knautia macedonica
Schizocodon soldanelloides magnus	Shortia soldanelloides var. magna
Scilla sibirica	Scilla siberica
Scrophularia aquatica variegata	Scrophularia auriculata 'Variegata'
Sedum maximum atro-purpureum	Sedum telephium subsp. maximum 'Atropurpureum'
Sedum spectabile Autumn Joy	Sedum 'Herbstfeude'
Sedum spectabile roseum	Sedum telephium 'Roseum'
Sedum spurium Schorbusser Blut	Sedum spurium 'Schorbuser Blut'
Senecio laxifolius	Brachyglottis 'Sunshine'
Senecio monroii	Brachyglottis monroi
Senecio smithii	Brachyglottis smithii
Shortia uniflora grandiflora	Shortia uniflora var. orbicularis 'Grandiflora'
Sibthorpia europaea variegata	Sibthorpia europaea 'Variegata'
Silene pendula compacta	Silene pendula 'Compacta'
Skimmia foremanii	Skimmia japonica 'Veitchii'
Spiraea aruncus	Aruncus dioicus
Stachys lanata	Stachys byzantina
Stachys macrantha superba	Stachys macrantha 'Superba'
Symphoricarpos orbiculatus variegatus	Symphoricarpos orbiculatus 'Foliis Variegatus'
Symphytum peregrinum	Symphytum x uplandicum
Symphytum x uplandicum variegatum	Symphytum x uplandicum 'Variegatum'
Taxus baccata repandens	Taxus baccata 'Repandens'
Tellima grandiflora purpurea	Tellima grandiflora Rubra Group
Tellima grandiflora rubra	Tellima grandiflora Rubra Group
Teucrium scordium crispum	Teucrium scorodonia 'Crispum'
Thalictrum adiantifolium	Thalictrum minus 'Adiantifolium'
Thalictrum glaucum	Thalictrum flavum subsp. glaucum
Thalictrum majus	Thalictrum aquilegiifolium
Thalictrum minus	Thalictrum aquilegiifolium
Thalictrum speciosissimum	Thalictrum flavum subsp. glaucum
Thermopsis montana	Thermopsis rhombifolia var. montana

Thymus azoricus	Thymus caespititius
Thymus x citriodorus aureus	Thymus pulegoides 'Aureus'
Thymus hirsutus doerfleri	Thymus doerfleri
Thymus lanuginosus	Thymus pseudolanuginosus
Thymus nitidus	Thymus richardii subsp. nitidus
Thymus serpyllum coccineus	Thymus 'Coccineus'
Thymus serpyllum lanuginosus	Thymus pseudolanuginosus
Thymus vulgaris aureus	Thymus pulegoides 'Goldentime'
Trifolium repens pentaphyllum	Trifolium repens 'Quinquefolium'
Trollius Alabaster	Trollius x cultorum 'Albaster'
Trollius europaeus superba	Trollius europaeus 'Superbus'
Trollius Orange Globe	Trollius x cultorum 'Orange Globe'
Ulex nanus	Ulex minor
Vaccinium vitis-idaea minus	Vaccinium vitis-idaea var. minus
Verbascum Broussa	Verbascum bombyciferum
Veronica catarractae	Parahebe catarractae
Veronica incana Wendy	Veronica spicata subsp. incana 'Wendy'
Veronica pectinata rosea	Veronica pectinata 'Rosea'
Veronica saxatilis	Veronica fruticans
Vinca acutiloba	Vinca difformis
Vinca major elegantissima	Vinca major 'Variegata'
Vinca minor argenteo-variegata	Vinca minor 'Argenteovariegata'
Vinca minor aureo-variegata	Vinca minor 'Aureovariegata'
Vinca minor caeruleo-plena	Vinca minor 'Azurea Flore Pleno'
Vinca minor Graveana	Vinca minor 'La Grave'
Vinca minor Miss Jekyll's Form	Vinca minor 'Gertrude Jekyll'
Vinca minor Mr Bowles' Form	Vinca minor 'La Grave'
Vinca minor multiplex	Vinca minor 'Multiplex'
Vinca minor punicea	Vinca minor 'Atropurpurea'
Vinca minor rubra	Vinca minor 'Atropurpurea'
Vinca minor variegata	Vinca minor 'Argenteovariegata'
Viola Admiral Avellan	Viola 'Ameril Avellan'
Viola cornuta alba	Viola cornuta Alba Group
Viola Princess of Wales	Viola 'Princesse de Galles'

Index

An * indicates a plant that is mentioned in the Plant-Name Changes section.